Microprocessor
Fundamentals

Microprocessor Fundamentals

Fred Halsall

MSc, DPhil, CEng, MIEE
Lecturer in electronics and computer science

Paul Lister

MSc, PhD, CEng, MIEE, MIEEE
Lecturer in electronics and control

University of Sussex UK
School of Engineering and Applied Sciences

Pitman

PITMAN BOOKS LIMITED
128 Long Acre, London WC2E 9AN

Associated Companies
Pitman Publishing New Zealand Ltd, Wellington
Pitman Publishing Pty Ltd, Melbourne

Printed and bound in Great Britain
at The Pitman Press, Bath

ISBN 0 273 01522 2

Contents

Preface

The wide range of application areas of microprocessors has resulted in many potential users of these devices having no previous knowledge of computer hardware or software (programming). It is for this reason that this book has been written as a basic introductory text on microprocessors and their applications, intended primarily for readers who have no previous knowledge in this field.

Generally, the many books currently available on microprocessors assume that the reader has a significant background knowledge of either digital hardware or software. Our approach has been to attempt to present the essential character of microprocessors and some of their associated application principles without resort to excessive electrical detail. Our experience of both teaching undergraduates and retraining engineers from industry is that an introduction to microprocessor applications can be taught effectively with little reference to hardware detail. This means that a broad spectrum of engineers, from many different backgrounds, can see the relevance of microprocessors to their speciality without having to master a wide range of electronics.

We have tried to present the material in this way with the supplementary objective of producing a volume that was not of a deterrent size or price.

There are now many students in technical colleges, polytechnics and universities being introduced to microprocessors at a very early stage in their studies and consequently the approach we have taken makes this book particularly suitable for recommendation for such courses.

The book has been written to be read on its own but many of the examples have been developed with a "hands-on" experience programme in mind using a single-board prototyping system. We have been involved in the preparation and presentation of a number of "hands-on" introductory courses on microprocessors and many of the program examples have been developed as a result of this experience. The microprocessor referred to throughout the book is the Intel 8085. This device is compatible in many respects with the earlier Intel 8080 and the derivative Zilog Z80 microprocessors and has become an industry standard 8-bit microprocessor.

Most of the programs presented can be run, with little or no modification, on an Intel SDK85 single board computer or the MAT385 Microprocessor Applications Trainer manufactured by Feedback Instruments Ltd of Crowborough, UK.

The basic principles of operation of a digital computer and the associated terminology are presented in Chapter 1. The bus structure and elements of a microprocessor-based computer are then introduced in Chapter 2. Chapters 3, 4 and 5 introduce the range of instructions and associated programming techniques typically available with microprocessors. The elements of digital input and output using a programmable input/output device are covered in Chapter 6. Analogue input and output techniques are introduced in Chapter 7. In Chapter 8 a range of simple application examples are presented that exploit many of the principles and techniques discussed in the earlier chapters.

The book attempts to illustrate the fundamental characteristics which are applicable to any microprocessor by continual reference to a typical one, thus avoiding the potentially confusing necessity to describe the many small differences between one microprocessor and another. An appendix has, however, been included which gives a brief summary of some of the main features of some of the other popular microprocessors which are currently available and, where appropriate, to indicate how they differ from the Intel 8085.

Dr F Halsall
Dr P F Lister
University of Sussex

To Rhiannon, Lisa, Richard, Muriel, Jenny and Ben

1 Computer Principles

1.1 Technology

The microprocessor is the culmination of the developments which have been taking place in semiconductor technology since the first production transistors produced in the early 1950s. Basically, a transistor is produced by adding impurities to a semiconducting material, usually silicon. It was soon realised that, by adding impurities to different areas of the same piece of silicon, it was possible to produce a number of interconnected transistors on the same silicon "chip". This became known as an **integrated circuit**.

Digital integrated circuits in the early 1960s involved small-scale integration (SSI), a typical circuit being a few logic gates. Later came medium-scale integration (MSI) with a complete integrated circuit counter or register possible. Further refinements and changes in technology have resulted in large-scale integration (LSI) devices being commercially available at low cost which are comprised of more than 10 000 individual transistors on a single silicon chip.

In order that such a circuit is widely applicable it must be very flexible; hence manufacturers have made these devices into *parts* of a digital computer. A microprocessor is one such device that forms the central part of a computer. Others include memory devices and programmable input/output circuits. All these devices are produced using the same semiconductor technology. The process consists of several stages of exposing intricate patterns on regions on the surface of the integrated circuit chip to gaseous impurities at high temperature. These regions are defined by a photographic procedure. The impurities form the various parts of a transistor that are finally interconnected by a metallisation layer that is etched into the conductor paths by a further photographic process.

A photomicrograph of a typical microprocessor chip is shown in Fig. 1.1. After fabrication, the integrated circuit chip is mounted onto a flat base containing a number of connection pins, and the terminal

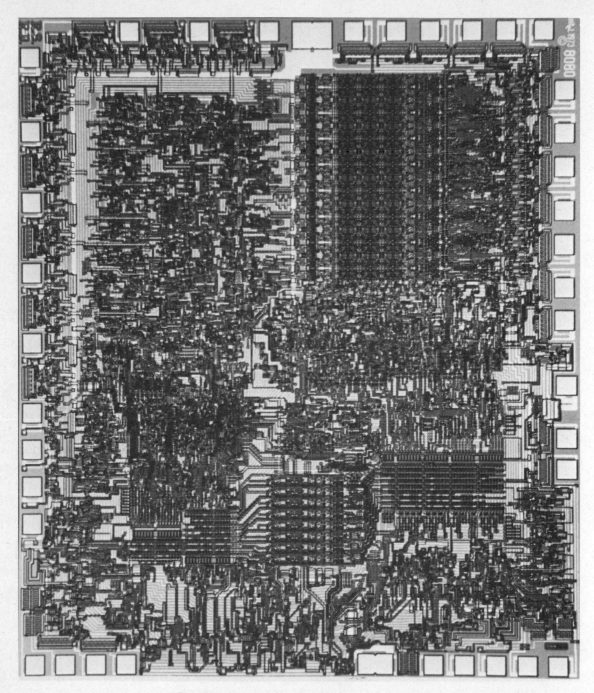

Fig. 1.1 Photomicrograph of a microprocessor (*Courtesy Intel Corp.*)
(Approx. size 5 mm square by 1 mm thick)

Fig. 1.2 A microprocessor, memory, and programmable input/output device (Approx. 1½ times actual size)

areas on the chip are connected to the corresponding pins on the base by means of small gold wires. The entire assembly is then sealed to form an integrated circuit package.

A photograph showing a fully-packaged microprocessor is seen in Fig. 1.2 together with integrated circuit memory and programmable input/output devices. These three components can be used to form a complete and powerful computing system.

1.2 Historical Development

The basic structure and mode of operation of the first digital computer was proposed by the mathematician Charles Babbage in the late 1830s. However, it was not until transistors were used to build them did computers become sufficiently reliable for their full potential to begin to be explored.

Since the first transistor-based machine was produced, computers have been used in an increasing variety of applications. These range from very large systems such as those used by banks to maintain customer accounts to quite small systems that may, for example, be used by an individual to solve a complex engineering problem. The advent of the microprocessor, however, means that it is now possible to have the power of a computer in a single integrated circuit, and consequently the range of applications is now virtually unlimited. It is widely predicted that in the near future computers will be found in almost every area of human endeavour. It is now possible to use a microprocessor to control an automatic washing machine or a central heating system or to control the exhaust emission from a car or the operation of traffic lights – the list of possibilities is endless.

1.3 Mode of Operation

Basically, all digital computers operate in the same way which to a large extent is independent of the specific application to which they are being put. This arises because a computer – large or small – is a flexible general-purpose machine or device that can be arranged to solve or implement a particular task after it has been produced by the manufacturer.

A task is implemented by deciding the **sequence of operations** needed to perform it. Consider a basic electronic calculator which offers the user a variety of operations – add, subtract, multiply, etc. It is then up to the user to select the particular sequence of these operations necessary to solve a specific problem. Similarly a digital computer can perform a number of basic operations called **machine instructions** which the user selects and orders in a way which solves a particular problem. This sequential list of operations is referred to as a **program**.

An electronic calculator executes each of its basic operations in typically a few milliseconds. Consequently the time taken to solve a problem with a calculator is determined primarily by the rate at which the user keys in the individual operations. The intrinsically high speed of execution of each operation is therefore lost. A digital computer, however, utilises the very high speed of execution of each machine instruction – usually a few microseconds – by having the required sequence of instructions, or program, stored within the computer itself. This is known as the **stored program concept** and is the fundamental difference between a basic calculator and a computer system.

The information or data which is fed into a computer and the data which is subsequently output by the computer varies considerably with the wide variety of applications. In a mathematical application, the input and subsequent output information will perhaps be numerical, and the computer might simply perform some arithmetic operations on the input values. An application typical of those to which microprocessor based computers are put is, for example, a temperature-control system. Here the input data might be an indication of the controlled temperature and the output a signal to turn a heating element either on or off.

Irrespective of the application, however, within the computer itself the same means of storing and coding information is employed. In order to achieve high levels of accuracy this coding is based on the **binary** (two-symbol) system. Information stored using this system in an electronic circuit is capable of being precise. This is because the information is not dependent on the *exact* values of voltages and current in the circuit provided these parameters can be unambiguously interpreted as representing one or other of the two binary symbols. All input data fed into a computer must first be translated into a binary coded form, and similarly the subsequent binary coded output must also be translated into the required form.

1.4 The Binary System

The binary system can perhaps be best explained by first considering a typical number in the decimal system. This system uses ten symbols, 0–9. The value of a symbol is weighted by its position in relation to other symbols making up a number:

$$10^4 \quad 10^3 \quad 10^2 \quad 10^1 \quad 10^0 \quad \text{weighting}$$
$$4 \quad 9 \quad 5 \quad 3 \quad 6 \quad \text{example}$$

Thus $49536 = 4 \times 10^4 + 9 \times 10^3 + 5 \times 10^2 + 3 \times 10^1 + 6 \times 10^0$. Each of the five **digits** of this example is one of the ten symbols 0–9. The weighting of each digit is a power of ten determined by the digit position; hence decimal numbers have a **base** of ten.

Binary numbers are constructed in just the same way except that they have a base of two. There are consequently only two symbols, 0 and 1, and digit weightings are powers of two:

$$2^4 \quad 2^3 \quad 2^2 \quad 2^1 \quad 2^0 \quad \text{weighting}$$
$$1 \quad 0 \quad 1 \quad 1 \quad 1 \quad \text{example}$$

Thus $10111 = 1 \times 2^4 + 0 \times 2^3 + 1 \times 2^2 + 1 \times 2^1 + 1 \times 2^0$ which is equivalent to 23 in the decimal system.

All information within a digital computer is represented in a binary form – both the input data to be manipulated and the coded instructions which control the various machine operations. The number of *bi*nary dig*it*s or **bits** used to make up the basic unit of information in a computer varies from one machine to another: for example 4, 8, 16, 24 and 32 bits have all been used in different machines.

Microprocessor systems often use either 8 or 16 bits for the basic unit of information or **word**. An 8-bit group is referred to as a **byte**. So a 16-bit word is equivalent to two bytes.

When examining the operation of a microprocessor system, therefore, binary patterns are always being considered. This can be very tedious for the programmer who is, when communicating this information, prone to make errors. It is for these reasons that alternative methods are often used to convey binary information between humans.

The method used is to group a number of bits together and then represent that group with an equivalent coded number or character. The most commonly used method is **hexadecimal** (base 16) coding which is based on a 4-bit group. There are sixteen combinations of four binary digits and hence sixteen symbols or characters are required. The sixteen symbols used are the ten numeric digits 0–9 plus the six alphabetic characters A–F. The binary codes and corresponding hexadecimal symbols are shown in Table 1.1.

Table 1.1   Hexadecimal numbers

4-bit binary pattern	Hexadecimal symbol
0000	0
0001	1
0010	2
0011	3
0100	4
0101	5
0110	6
0111	7
1000	8
1001	9
1010	A
1011	B
1100	C
1101	D
1110	E
1111	F

Some examples of binary patterns and their equivalent hexadecimal (hex) representation are given below:

$$01101101 = 6D(\text{hex}) \qquad 11110010 = F2(\text{hex})$$
$$\quad 6 \quad D \qquad\qquad\qquad F \quad 2$$

$$1011010010001110 = B48E(\text{hex})$$
$$\quad B \quad 4 \quad 8 \quad E$$

1.5 Basic Structure and Operation

A digital computer executes a list of basic machine instructions (a program) which have been selected and ordered by the user to solve a particular task. In order to exploit the intrinsic high speed of execution of each machine instruction, the program is stored within the computer. In addition, all information stored within the computer – both machine instructions and data – is represented in a binary coded form. Thus a basic digital computer is comprised of a **memory** which is primarily used to hold or store the program, a **microprocessor** (often referred to as the central processor unit or CPU) which executes the individual machine instructions which make up the program, and some **input and output** (I/O) **ports**. These ports form the **interface** between the computer and the source of the input data and the subsequent output data. The complete combination of microprocessor, memory and input and output ports is collectively referred to as a **microcomputer** and is illustrated in Fig. 1.3.

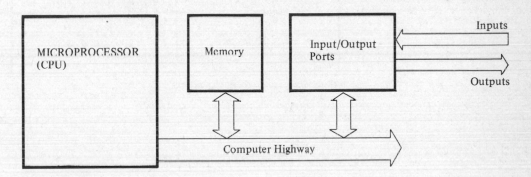

Fig. 1.3 A microcomputer

Once the program has been evolved for the task, the complete program is loaded into memory and is then executed. During program execution, each machine instruction is accessed sequentially from the memory and then executed by the microprocessor. The microprocessor therefore operates in a two phase mode: during the first phase, the **fetch cycle**, the next instruction is fetched from memory; then, in the second phase or **execution cycle**, the microprocessor executes (or performs) the action specified by the instruction.

In order to remember which program instruction is to be executed next, the microprocessor contains a register (or temporary information storage location) called the **program counter** (PC), the contents of which points to the next sequential instruction to be fetched and executed. Thus, during a typical instruction cycle, the next instruction to be executed is read from the memory location indicated by the contents of the program counter. While this instruction is being

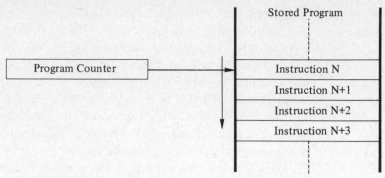

a) The Program Counter Register

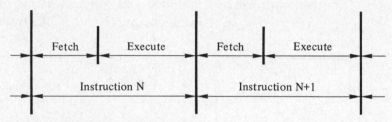

b) Fetch-Execute Mode of Operation

Fig. 1.4 Program execution

executed, the contents of the program counter are incremented to point to the next instruction. This is summarised in Fig. 1.4.

Microprocessor instructions often require more than one byte of information; usually 1, 2 or 3 bytes are required. Thus an instruction fetch cycle may consist of up to 3 memory read operations performed on successive memory locations. During the execution phase of this instruction however, the program counter still points to the address of the first byte of the instruction that would normally be fetched next.

Exercises

1.1 Convert the following decimal numbers into their equivalent binary numbers:

    35   67   224

1.2 Convert the following binary numbers into their equivalent decimal numbers:

    10111   1010101   11011011

1.3 Convert the following decimal numbers into their equivalent hexadecimal number:

    27   96   3334

1.4 Convert the following hexadecimal numbers into their equivalent decimal numbers:

    C3   · 2F   2C9E

2 Microcomputer Architecture

2.1 Introduction

The basic functional units of a microcomputer were discussed in Chapter 1. These comprise the microprocessor itself (the CPU), the memory which is used primarily to hold the stored program, and some input and output ports which are used to interface the microcomputer to the various input and output devices controlled by it.

2.2 The Microprocessor

The microprocessor can execute a number of basic machine instructions. Examples are individual data byte manipulation instructions (add, subtract, etc.) and memory transfer instructions (read data byte from memory, write data byte to memory, etc.). Information is transferred between external devices and the computer system via the input and output ports, and consequently the microprocessor has machine instructions to both read (input) data from a specified port and to write (output) data to a port.

Basically a microprocessor is comprised, as far as a user is concerned, of the three sections shown in Fig. 2.1.

The **register** section contains a number of registers or temporary storage elements which can each hold or store a single byte or word. The **arithmetic logic unit** (ALU) performs the actual data manipulation operations, and the **timing and control** section co-ordinates the internal operation of the microprocessor and controls operation of the ALU and registers so that the desired action specified by an instruction is performed.

The microprocessor communicates with the memory, both to obtain the individual instructions which make up the program and to access and store data, and to transfer data to and from input and output ports using a **highway** or **bus**.

More detail about the various microprocessor registers and their use will be given in the next chapter.

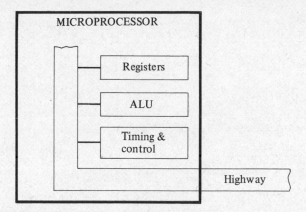

Fig. 2.1 A basic microprocessor

2.3 Memory

The memory consists of a number of **locations** each individually identified by an **address**. Each location contains a binary pattern with a number of bits corresponding to the word length of the computer (typically 8 bits). The binary pattern stored at an address is referred to as the **contents** of that address. In a microprocessor system the memory is usually comprised of two types: **random access memory** (RAM) and **read only memory** (ROM). Basically RAM (more appropriately called read/write memory but universally referred to as RAM) has the capability of having information both written into and read out of each location and is often used for storing intermediate results (data) during a computation. ROM has information fixed into it either during its manufacture or by the user and consequently can only be operated in a read-only mode.

For many dedicated microprocessor applications ROM is used to hold the (fixed) program. It has the advantage of being **non-volatile** which means that when its power supplies are removed the stored information is not lost. RAM is normally *volatile* unless the special design features of certain types are exploited. The memory pattern programmed into a factory programmed ROM during its manufacture cannot be changed and hence it is essential that the program to be stored in it is correct and free from errors. This type of ROM is widely used in large-volume applications since the cost per bit is then very low.

Erasable programmable ROMs or EPROMs have a memory pattern which can be changed by the user in a controlled manner, and hence this is a particularly useful device during program development. The memory pattern in an EPROM is erased either by exposure to intensive ultraviolet light through a "window" on the

Fig. 2.2   A UV EPROM and PROM programmer
(*Courtesy Intel Corp.*)

integrated circuit itself – UV EPROM – or by applying a voltage to specific pins on the integrated circuit – EAROM or electrically alterable ROM. The new memory pattern is then written into the device using special hardware called a PROM programmer. An example of a UV EPROM and a commercially available PROM programmer is shown in Fig. 2.2.

2.4 Highway Structure

The computer highway consists of three separate buses: the data bus, the address bus, and the control bus. This is shown in Fig. 2.3.

The **data bus** is used to carry the data associated with a memory or input/output transfer and is typically 8 bits wide. The **address bus** is used to specify the memory location or input/output port involved in a transfer. The **control bus** is made up of the various control lines generated by the microprocessor and other system components to synchronise transfers.

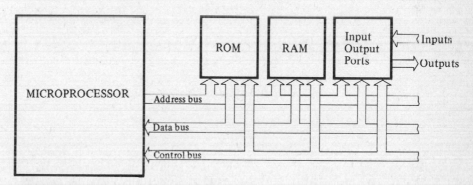

Fig. 2.3 Highway structure

The data bus of many computers and particularly microprocessor-based computers is bidirectional. That is, the processor can write data on to the bus lines to be read by, for example, a memory device or it can read data from the bus presented by such a device. Hence data can be transferred from the processor to a device or from a device to the processor over a single set of data lines. This is a particularly desirable mechanism in a microprocessor system since it is not necessary for the microprocessor to have both data input and output pins. A practical limit to the number of available pins on a microprocessor integrated circuit makes it important for the manufacturer to use those available efficiently.

It becomes possible to make a single pin a logic input and output by incorporating, within the microprocessor logic output gates, a third output state in addition to the normal 0 and 1 signals. This third state is a high impedance condition where the output is effectively

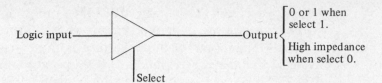

Fig. 2.4   A three-state output

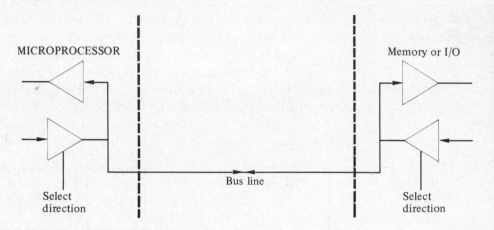

Fig. 2.5   A bidirectional bus line

switched off. A select input to the gate is used to force the output to this off state. This is illustrated in Fig. 2.4.

Devices of this type can be used to form a bidirectional bus by connecting them in the arrangement shown in Fig. 2.5. This is for a single line of a bus.

The microprocessor end of the bus can be either an input or an output (but not both simultaneously) depending on the direction selection control. The same applies to the memory or input/output end of the bus. Control signals ensure that the direction of data flow at each end of the bus is synchronised.

The address bus consists typically of 16 lines on which a binary coded address can be presented to a memory or input/output port. The range of possible addresses is therefore from 0000 (hex) to FFFF (hex), i.e. 65 536 (decimal) separate addresses. Thus a typical micro-processor can address up to 65 536 (decimal) memory locations each containing 8 bits (or one byte) of information. The size of a computer memory is often measured in units of **1024** (decimal) locations. This unit is designated **1K**. Hence most microprocessor systems can have a maximum of 64K memory locations ($64 \times 1024 = 65\ 536$).

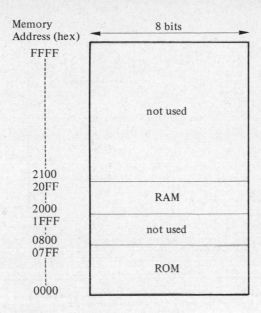

Fig. 2.6 A typical memory map

2.5 Memory Map

For many microprocessor applications it is not necessary to use all the possible memory addresses in the system. The range of addresses that are used and the type of memory in each range is indicated by a **memory map**. A memory map for a small but typical microcomputer system is shown in Fig. 2.6. The figure shows that the system has 2K (0000 → 07FF) bytes of ROM and 256 (2000 → 20FF) bytes of RAM.

In a small system of this type it is possible to allocate some of the unused addresses to input/output ports. Data can then be transferred between the microprocessor and an input/output port using the same machine instructions as are used for transferring data between the microprocessor and a memory location. This technique is discussed in Chapter 6.

2.6 Address Decoding

Since there are a number of devices connected to the computer highway – ROM and RAM chips, input/output devices, etc. – it is necessary to ensure that only the device intended for the data transfer responds when a request is made by the microprocessor. This is accomplished by each device connected to the highway having a **chip-select** (CS) control input, and only when this input is activated

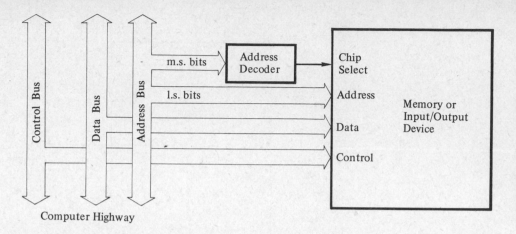

Fig. 2.7 Address decoding

does a device respond to the various requests issued on the control bus.

The memory map, as previously described, is used to define the address range of each device connected to the bus. Each device, therefore, has an additional logic circuit associated with it which detects when an address intended for that device is present on the bus. This is known as an address decoder and its output is used to activate the chip-select input of the device.

In practice only the most significant address bits need be decoded since the least significant address bits are used by the device itself to determine, for example, the specific location within the selected memory device. This is shown in Fig. 2.7.

2.7 Bus Control   The control bus incorporates the **timing signals** which are generated by the microprocessor to synchronise information transfers between the microprocessor and a memory or input/output port. Consider the timing diagram shown in Fig. 2.8.

The figure illustrates the two control signals – read (RD) and write (WR) – generated by the microprocessor during two successive instruction cycles. The example assumes both are single byte instructions: the first is a memory (or input port) read and the second is a memory (or output port) write. The type of transfer – memory or input/output – will be determined by the memory map and the specific address output by the microprocessor during each execute cycle.

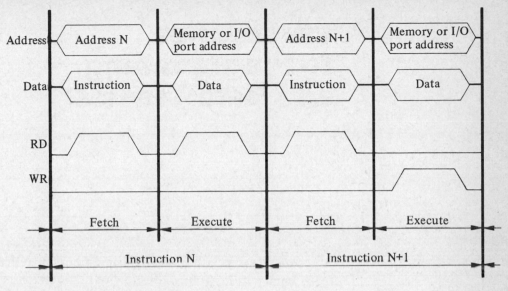

Fig. 2.8 Timing diagram

Exercises

2.1 Determine the maximum memory space for an 8-bit microprocessor which has a 14-bit address word. Express your answer in K bytes.

2.2 A microcomputer system requires 4K bytes of ROM and 256 bytes of RAM. Determine the start and end addresses of each memory block if the two memories are to occupy contiguous blocks of memory starting at address 0000 hex. Express your answer in hex notation.

2.3 If the microcomputer system in 2.2 requires four additional input/output ports, define suitable addresses for the ports assuming memory-mapped input/output.

2.4 A microcomputer system has the following memory map:

$$0000 \rightarrow 0FFF \quad ROM$$
$$2000 \rightarrow 21FF \quad RAM$$
$$4000 \rightarrow 400F \quad I/O$$

Determine the amount of ROM and RAM memory and the number of I/O ports in the system.

3 Introduction to Programming and Data Transfer

3.1 Introduction

A microcomputer can conveniently be considered as a device which reads binary coded information from its input ports, manipulates this information according to a program stored within its memory, and subsequently produces output information at its output ports. This is illustrated in Fig. 3.1.

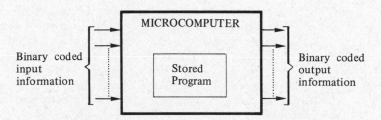

Fig. 3.1 A microcomputer

The instructions which make up the program are those selected by the programmer from the instruction set of the microprocessor in order to perform the required task. Before a programmer is able to either write or interpret the meaning of a program, it is necessary to become familiar with the different types of machine instructions which a typical microprocessor executes and to investigate their effect on the total system. The aim of this chapter therefore is to introduce the different types of machine instructions which are typically available and to show how some simple programs can be evolved using some of these instructions.

The microprocessor selected for example purposes in this and subsequent chapters is the Intel 8085. This is a widely used device and its architecture and instruction set are typical of an 8-bit microprocessor.

**3.2 Microprocessor
Registers**

The majority of machine instructions available with a microprocessor operate on or affect the state of various internal registers which make up the microprocessor. Before a program can be written for a particular microprocessor, therefore, it is necessary to acquire a knowledge of those processor registers which are accessible or are affected by the machine instructions. The main registers for the Intel 8085, for example, are as shown in Fig. 3.2.

Further explanation and use of these registers will be given as the various machine instructions are introduced in this and subsequent chapters.

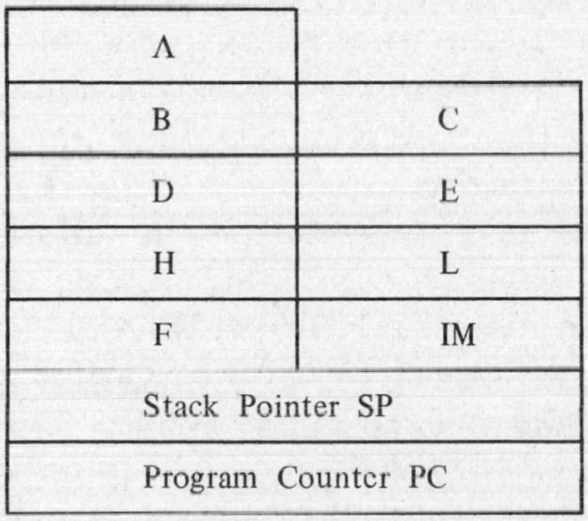

A	
B	C
D	E
H	L
F	IM
Stack Pointer SP	
Program Counter PC	

A   is an 8-bit arithmetic register (accumulator).

B, C, D, E   are four 8-bit general purpose registers.

F   is an 8-bit flags register (modified by ALU operations).

IM   is an 8-bit interrupt control register.

HL   are two 8-bit registers which are normally used to form a 16-bit memory pointer.

SP   is the stack pointer register — this contains a 16-bit memory address which displays points to the top of a system stack.

PC   is the program counter register which contains a 16-bit memory address which points to the next instruction to be executed.

Fig. 3.2   Main registers in the Intel 8085

3.3 Assembly Language

It is extremely tedious and time consuming to represent each machine instruction in its binary coded form. A far more convenient representation of an instruction is what is known as its **symbolic assembly language** equivalent. When each instruction is represented in this form, programs are far more readable (and hence understandable) but, since there is a one-for-one correspondence between an assembly language instruction and a machine code instruction, it is also very straightforward to convert between one form and the other. All the programs which are presented in this and subsequent chapters will be written in assembly language. The method used to convert these to basic machine language form is described later in this chapter.

A typical assembly language instruction has the following **format**:

LABEL: OPERATION MNEMONIC, OPERANDS COMMENTS

The LABEL is an optional symbolic address for the instruction which, as will be seen in Chapter 6, is particularly useful for branch-type instructions.

Each machine instruction is assigned a corresponding OPERATION MNEMONIC which effectively tells the programmer the specific operation to be performed. OPERANDS is either a value on which this operation is to be carried out or the memory location(s) where the value(s) can be found.

The COMMENTS field is for optional comments and is simply to facilitate understanding and enhance the readability of the complete program and does not influence the machine code resulting from the assembly instruction.

3.4 Classification of Instructions

Although a microprocessor may execute perhaps a hundred or more different machine instructions, each instruction can in general be classified as being a member of one of just five groups. These groups are

Data Transfer
Data Manipulation
Transfer of Control
Input/Output
Machine Control

Instructions in the **data transfer** group move data between the various processor registers or between a processor register and a memory location. For example,

MOV   A, B

results in the contents of the B-register being transferred to the A-register.

Instructions in the **data manipulation** group perform arithmetic and logical operations on data which is either in a specified processor register or a memory location. For example,

ADD   A, B

results in the A-register (accumulator) containing the sum of its previous contents and the contents of the B-register. All instructions in this group normally modify processor flags.

Instructions in the **transfer of control** group include unconditional and conditional (flag dependent) jump instructions and subroutine call and return instructions. All instructions in this group act on the program counter and indeed it is this group of instructions which gives the stored program machine its great flexibility. For example,

JMP   LABEL1

results in the microprocessor breaking its normal mode of sequential instruction execution and instead jumping unconditionally to symbolic address LABEL1 for the next instruction to be executed.

Instructions in the **input/output** group move data between the various input/output ports of the system and an internal processor register – usually the A-register. For example,

OUT   05

results in the contents of the A-register being transferred to output port 05(hex).

Instructions in the **machine control** group affect the state or mode of operation of the processor itself. Some examples to be discussed include interrupt enable and disable, processor halt (wait for an interrupt), and no operation instructions.

3.5 Operand Addressing Modes

A typical machine instruction implies three addresses: two to specify the location of the values to be manipulated (the source addresses) and the third to specify the location where the result is to be stored (the destination address):

Source 1
Operation → Destination
Source 2

In order to reduce the number of different addresses required for an instruction, however, if two source addresses are required the destination address is usually the same as one of the sources. Consequently, most microprocessors – including the Intel 8085 – only require a maximum of two addresses to be specified.

The above examples show that the specific source and destination addresses used vary for different types of instruction. Data movement instructions, for example, utilise the various processor registers or memory locations as source and destination addresses, whilst other instructions may typically specify an actual data value in place of an address.

The type of source and destination addresses utilised by an instruction is determined by the **instruction addressing mode** and all microprocessors provide a variety of different addressing modes. The range of addressing modes provided by a particular microprocessor is important since it can often result in considerable flexibility when writing a program and also leads to programs which require fewer instructions to implement a given task.

The four main types of addressing modes used in microprocessor systems are:

Register Addressing
Immediate Addressing
} These are used primarily for data transfer and manipulation instructions which involve only the internal processor registers.

Direct (Extended) Addressing
Register Indirect Addressing
} These are used primarily for data transfer and manipulation instructions which involve the system memory.

In order to give examples of the use of each of these types of addressing modes, in this chapter we will consider some examples of instructions from the data transfer group. Subsequent chapters will introduce instructions from the other groups.

3.6 Data Transfer Instructions

Perhaps the most basic machine instructions are those from the data transfer group. These are generally referred to as the move or load instructions and some examples using each of the above addressing modes are described below.

3.6.1 Register Addressing

This mode is used to move data between the internal processor registers, and hence the instruction source and destination addresses specify which of these registers are involved in the transfer.

For example:

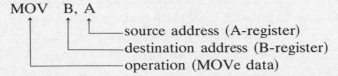

MOV   B, A

— source address (A-register)
— destination address (B-register)
— operation (MOVe data)

This results in the contents of the A-register being transferred to the B-register. The contents of the A-register remain unchanged. This is often written as:

$(B) \leftarrow (A)$

where the brackets mean "contents of".

Another example:

MOV   C, B

means move or transfer the contents of the B-register to the C-register:

$(C) \leftarrow (B)$

In addition, there are a limited number of data transfer instructions which involve combined 16-bit register pairs – for example, DE and HL. A typical instruction is

XCHG

This results in the contents of register pair DE being exchanged with the contents of register pair HL. This can be represented as

$(DE) \leftrightarrow (HL)$

3.6.2   Immediate Addressing

With this mode, the source address does not specify a register or memory location but instead the actual source *data* is contained within the instruction itself and is therefore immediately available.

For example:

MVI   A,   FE(hex)

— source *data*
— destination address
— operation

This results in the data value FE(hex) in this example being transferred to the A-register:

$(A) \leftarrow FE(hex)$

or $A \leftarrow 11111110(binary)$

Similarly, a 16-bit register pair (BC, DE or HL) may be specified as the destination address and consequently these instructions require two bytes of immediate data.

For example:

LXI   H,   802D

This results in the 16-bit register pair HL being loaded with immediate data 802D(hex):

(H)(L) ← 802D(hex)

Another example:

LXI   D,   E627

which means

(D)(E) ← E627(hex)

i.e. registers D and E are loaded as a pair.

Program Example 3.1:   Register Data Transfer

The program example of Fig. 3.3 uses a combination of the above instructions. The program loads a value into the A-register using immediate addressing and then loads this value into two further registers, B and C, using register addressing. Finally, register pairs HL and DE are loaded using immediate addressing and their contents exchanged using register addressing.

Assembly Instructions			COMMENTS*
MNEMONIC	OP1	OP2	
MVI	A	FE	(A) ← FE (hex)
MOV	B	A	(B) ← (A)
MOV	C	B	(C) ← (B)
LXI	H	802D	(H) (L) ← 802D (hex)
LXI	D	E627	(D) (E) ← E627 (hex)
XCHG			(D) (E) ↔ (H) (L)

Fig. 3.3 Program Example 3.1

*The COMMENTS field is not used, in normal programming practice, to explain the action of an instruction which is assumed understood.

3.6.3   Direct Addressing

Using direct addressing, an operand may be either read from or written to a memory location, the address of which is specified in the instruction itself. Since all memory addresses are 16-bits, the address requires two bytes and it is for this reason that this mode is often referred to as extended addressing.

For example: LDA   20EA

This results in the A-register being loaded with the contents of the memory location with address 20EA(hex) and is expressed as

   (A) ← (20EA)

Similarly, the contents of the A-register may be stored in a specified memory location.

For example: STA   20F2

This results in the contents of the A-register being stored in memory location 20F2(hex) and is expressed as

   (20F2) ← (A)

As the next section will show, the register pair H and L is frequently used to hold a combined 16-bit memory address and consequently two instructions are provided to enable the two registers (H and L) to be loaded using a single instruction and direct addressing:

For example: LHLD   20A2

This results in register L being loaded with the contents of memory location 20A2 and register H being loaded with the contents of the next consecutive memory location, i.e. 20A3 in this example. This is therefore expressed as

   (L) ← (20A2)

   (H) ← (20A3)

Similarly   SHLD   20AF

This results in the current contents of register L being stored in memory location 20AF and the contents of register H being stored in memory location 20B0. This is expressed as

   (20AF) ← (L)

   (20B0) ← (H)

Assembly Instructions	Action
MVI A, FF	(A) ← FF (hex)
STA 20A2	(20A2) ← (A)
MVI A, EE	(A) ← EE (hex)
STA 20A3	(20A3) ← (A)
LHLD 20A2	(L) ← (20A2) i.e. FF (hex)
	(H) ← (20A3) i.e. EE (hex)
SHLD 20A4	(20A4) ← (L)
	(20A5) ← (H)

Fig. 3.4 Program Example 3.2

Program Example 3.2:   Direct Addressing

The program of Fig. 3.4 uses a combination of immediate and direct addressing, first to store immediate data into two consecutive memory locations, then to load register pair HL with this data, and finally to store the same data into a pair of different memory locations.

3.6.4   Register Indirect Addressing

Using direct addressing, only the A-register may be used to store or load a value to or from memory. Thus if a value were to be stored in a memory location from, say, the B-register, using direct addressing, it would first be necessary to transfer the contents from B to A before the store operation could be performed. A more efficient method, therefore, is to use register indirect addressing since, with this mode, data may be transferred between any of the processor registers and the system memory.

Using register indirect addressing, the operand is either read from or written to the memory location, the address of which is currently stored in the register pair HL. The instruction does not contain the actual memory address itself, therefore, but instead *implies* that the address to be used is currently stored in the HL register pair. The actual memory address is therefore obtained *indirectly*.

For example: MOV A, M

This results in the A-register being loaded with the contents of the memory location whose address is specified in registers H and L. This is represented as

$$(A) \leftarrow ((H)(L))$$

Similarly   MOV M, B

This results in the contents of the B-register being transferred to the memory location whose address is in registers H and L. This is represented as

$$((H)(L)) \leftarrow (B)$$

In addition to being able to load immediate data into a specified processor register, there is also an instruction to enable immediate data to be stored directly into a memory location. Again the memory address is stored in the register pair H and L. Thus

MVI M, FF

results in the value FF(hex) being stored in the memory location whose address is in registers H and L. This is represented as

$$((H)(L)) \leftarrow FF(hex)$$

Program Example 3.3: *Register Indirect Addressing*

The program of Fig. 3.5 uses a combination of immediate and register indirect addressing. A memory address is first loaded into registers H and L using immediate addressing and then a value is loaded into this memory location using register indirect addressing. Finally, the value is loaded into two further registers again using register indirect addressing.

Assembly Instructions	Action
LXI H, 20A0	(L) ← A0 (hex)
	(H) ← 20 (hex)
MVI M, AA	((H) (L)) ← AA (hex) i.e. (20A0) ← AA (hex)
MOV B, M	(B) ← (20A0) i.e. (B) ← AA(hex)
MOV C, M	(C) ← (20A0) i.e. (C) ← AA(hex)

Fig. 3.5 Program Example 3.3

3.7 The Intel 8085 Instruction Set

The instructions which have so far been introduced are by no means the only instructions available in the data transfer group. Indeed, they are intended only as examples from the complete list of instructions which is available. For instance, in the data transfer group there are instructions to enable data to be transferred (moved) between any pair of processor registers selected from A, B, C, D, E, H and L. Similarly, immediate data may be loaded into each of these registers.

The aim of this and subsequent chapters is simply to introduce examples of instructions from a particular instruction group, together with their meaning and application areas, so that the reader is able firstly to understand the function of each particular instruction group and secondly to select those instructions from the group which are required to perform a specific task. The complete list of instructions which comprise the Intel 8085 instruction set is given in Appendix 1.

3.8 The Assembly Process

A microprocessor executes instructions which are stored as binary-coded numbers in its program memory. Consequently, before any programs can be executed, including the examples above, they must first be converted from symbolic assembly to the equivalent binary form.

General purpose computer systems, whether mainframe, minicomputer or microprocessor based systems, usually incorporate a suite of programs (system programs) which have been designed to translate programs written in higher-level languages (source code) into machine (object) code.

If a line of source program in a high level language (e.g. Fortran) usually yields more than one machine instruction, this translation program is called a **compiler**. If the compiler program runs on one machine and generates machine code for another computer, it is referred to as a cross-compiler. The compilation process is illustrated in Fig. 3.6.

If a line of source program usually yields just one machine instruction, the translation process is called assembly and a program that performs this process is called an **assembler**. Cross-assemblers run on host machines and produce machine code output intended for another computer. Further aspects of systems programs are discussed in Chapter 9.

In many small microcomputer prototyping systems the resident operating program (monitor) cannot perform a complete translation process on an assembly language program and instead each instruction must first be converted into an intermediate hexadecimal form. The monitor then translates each pair of hexadecimal characters into

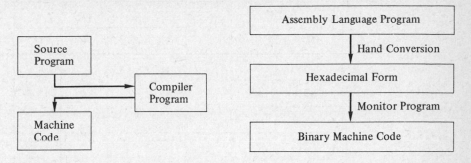

Fig. 3.6 The compilation process   **Fig. 3.7** The hand assembly process

the corresponding 8-bit binary pattern. Since the conversion from symbolic assembly form to hexadecimal has to be frequently performed by the programmer, the manufacturers list of machine instructions usually contains the corresponding hexadecimal code for each instruction. The hand assembly process is summarised in Fig. 3.7.

3.8.1 Hand Coding

The list of instructions for the Intel 8085 in Appendix 1 shows that each symbolic assembly language instruction requires from one to three bytes in hexadecimal form. For example, the instruction

    MOV A, B   (A) ← (B)

requires a single byte:

7   8

The instruction

    MVI A, FE   (A) ← FE(hex)

requires two bytes:

3E	Operation
FE	Immediate data, e.g. FE(hex)

Similarly, the instruction

    STA 20F2

requires three bytes:

32	Operation
F2	least significant byte of memory address
20	most significant byte of memory address

LINE No.	MEMORY		LABEL	ASSEMBLY			COMMENTS
	ADDRESS	CONT		MNEMONIC	OP1	OP2	
1	2000	3E		MVI	A	FE	(A) ← FE (hex)
	2001	FE					
2	2002	47		MOV	B	A	(B) ← (A)
3	2003	4F		MOV	C	B	(C) ← (B)
4	2004	21		LXI	H	802D	(H) (L) ← 802D (hex)
	2005	2D					
	2006	80					
5	2007	11		LXI	D	E627	(D) (E) ← E627 (hex)
	2008	27					
	2009	E6					
6	200A	EB		XCHG			(D) (E) → (H) (L)

Fig. 3.8 Hand coding example

As an example of the hand coding process, Fig. 3.8 shows program example 3.1 in both assembly language and hexadecimal form. The program is assumed to be stored in memory starting at address 2000(hex).

Exercises

3.1 Write an assembly language program to
i) load the B-register with immediate data 87(hex)
ii) transfer this value into registers A and C
iii) load the D-register with immediate data 2F(hex)
iv) transfer this value into register E
v) load the HL register pair with immediate data 8EF2(hex).

3.2 Write an assembly language program to:
i) load the A-register with immediate data FF(hex)
ii) store this in memory at location 20FF(hex) using direct addressing
iii) load register pair H and L with immediate data 20FF(hex)
iv) load the B-register with the previously stored data using register indirect addressing
v) transfer the data in the B-register to registers C and D using register addressing.

3.3 List the above programs on a table similar to that shown in figure 3.8 and obtain the hexadecimal code for each instruction using the information in Appendix 1.

3.4 Derive the contents of processor registers A, B and C and the contents of memory locations 2020, 2021 and 2080 after the following program has run and obtain the hexadecimal code for the program from Appendix 1.

```
LXI     H, 2020
LXI     D, 2080
XCHG
MVI     A, 2A
MOV     M, A
MVI     A, 20
MOV     B, A
XCHG
MOV     M, B
XCHG
MOV     C, M
MOV     A, C
STA     2021
HALT
```

4 Data Manipulation

4.1 Introduction

Since microprocessors may be used in a wide variety of applications, it is necessary to be able to represent data within a microcomputer in a number of different forms. For example, in some applications a simple unsigned binary representation is adequate but in others it may be advantageous to represent the data in a binary coded decimal form. This chapter, therefore, first describes the different methods available for representing data within a microcomputer, and then introduces some typical arithmetic instructions from the data manipulation group to illustrate their use with each form of number representation.

4.2 Data Representation

Before considering specific arithmetic instructions, it is necessary to examine the different ways numbers can be represented in a microcomputer. In general, numbers may be represented in unsigned binary, signed binary, or binary coded decimal (BCD) form. These are considered in turn.

4.2.1 Unsigned Binary

Unsigned binary is the most basic and, for microprocessors, the most common form of number representation. In this representation all numbers are assumed positive and a byte is simply the 8-bit binary equivalent of the number. Some examples follow:

2^7	2^6	2^5	2^4	2^3	2^2	2^1	2^0 = weighting
0	0	1	0	1	0	1	1 = 43 (decimal)
0	1	0	0	0	1	1	0 = 70
1	0	1	0	0	0	0	1 = 161
1	1	0	0	1	1	0	0 = 204

Thus the range of numbers (in unsigned binary form) for an 8-bit microprocessor using one byte per number is from 0 to 255; numbers in excess of 255 must therefore be represented by two or more bytes.

4.2.2 Signed Binary

For some applications it is necessary to be able to represent both positive and negative numbers. Moreover, when performing arithmetic operations on the numbers it is necessary to produce the correct signed result. Thus with a signed binary form of number representation, one bit, usually the most significant, is used to indicate the sign of the number.

The simplest form of signed binary representation is **sign and magnitude** since in this form the most significant bit indicates the sign (0 positive, 1 negative) and the other seven bits the magnitude.

For example: 0   0011010 = +26
                 1   1100100 = −100

Unfortunately, however, with this form it is not possible to perform simple arithmetic operations on numbers and automatically produce the correct signed result. It is for this reason that the **two's complement** form of representation is often used because, as will be shown later, performing arithmetic operations on two's complement signed numbers automatically produces the correct two's complement signed result.

As before, with two's complement the most significant bit, S, of each number is used as a sign bit:

m.s.   l.s.

| S | 6 | 5 | 4 | 3 | 2 | 1 | 0 |

S = 0 for positive numbers and zero

S = 1 for negative numbers

For positive numbers, the simple binary codes is used to represent the number. For negative numbers, however, the number is represented in its two's complement form. To obtain the two's complement of a number, the number is first inverted (complemented) and the resulting number incremented by 1.

For example: Another example:

$+15 = 00001111$ $+89 = 01011001$
⎞ invert ⎞ invert
11110000⎟ 10100110⎟
⎟ increment ⎟ increment
$-15 = 11110001$⎠ $-89 = 10100111$⎠

Note that, after the complement process, the most significant bit is automatically a 1. For an 8-bit microprocessor, therefore, the range of possible one byte numbers is summarised in the Table 4.1.

Table 4.1 Two's Complement Representation

Decimal number	Two's complement representation
+127	01111111
.	.
.	.
.	.
+3	00000011
+2	00000010
+1	00000001
0	00000000
−1	11111111
−2	11111110
−3	11111101
.	.
.	.
.	.
−127	10000001
−128	10000000

Note from the table that the maximum positive number that can be represented is +127 and the maximum negative number is −128. When performing arithmetic operations on 8-bit two's complement signed numbers, therefore, it is important not to exceed this range, otherwise incorrect answers will be obtained. For example, $(+68) + (+76)$ will produce an incorrect result since the result $(+144)$ exceeds the maximum possible positive number with 8-bits $(+127)$. Similarly, $(-68) - (+76)$ will also produce an incorrect result since the result (-144) is more than the maximum possible negative number (-128).

4.2.3 Binary Coded Decimal (BCD)

It is sometimes preferable in some applications to use decimal number representation and arithmetic within the microcomputer; for example, if the input data is from a decimal keypad and the subsequent output data drives a decimal display. Most microcomputers, therefore, provide instructions for performing arithmetic on **binary coded decimal** (BCD) numbers. BCD representation is a subset of the hexadecimal system introduced earlier and is summarised in the

Table 4.2 BCD Code

Decimal digit	BCD code
0	0000
1	0001
2	0010
3	0011
4	0100
5	0101
6	0110
7	0111
8	1000
9	1001

Table 4.2. Thus an 8-bit binary number may be used to store two BCD characters.

For example: $1000\ 0110 = 86$ (decimal)

$0101\ 0001 - 51$ (decimal)

Summarising, the programmer may choose one of three different forms of number representation. It should be stressed, however, that the type of representation being used is in many ways transparent to the microprocessor since this simply treats the data as an 8-bit binary pattern and it is the responsibility of the programmer to process and interpret this data in a form necessary to solve the particular task.

4.3 Arithmetic Instructions

The basic arithmetic instructions provided by a microcomputer are add, subtract, increment, and decrement. In general, with the 8085, these instructions always involve the A-register and either another processor register or a memory location. Since programmers may require to interpret the data within the microcomputer in dissimiliar ways, a microprocessor contains a number of different forms of these instructions so that data can be manipulated in the selected manner. In addition, the microprocessor contains a number of **flags** (status or condition bits) which are either set or reset depending on the particular arithmetic instruction being carried out and the programmer is

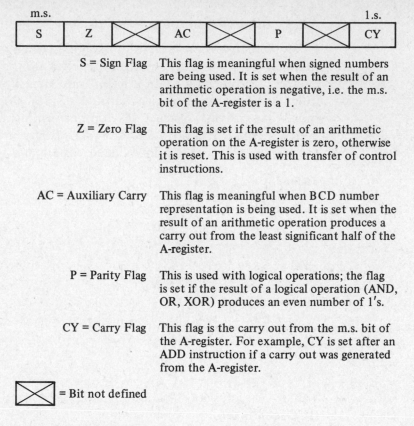

Fig. 4.1 8085 flags register

able to use and interpret these flags in order to manipulate data in the selected way.

The individual flag bits are grouped together to form the flag register, F, and as an example the F-register for the 8085 is shown in Fig. 4.1.

Some examples of arithmetic instructions are now given together with their effect on the individual flags in the flag register.

4.3.1 Add Instructions

The addition of two bits is summarised by the Table 4.3.

Table 4.3 shows that, because the sum can only be 0 or 1, a carry may be generated which must be added to the next higher order pair

Table 4.4 Addition of Two Bits and a Carry-in

Bit 1	Bit 2	Carry-in	Sum	Carry-out
0	0	0	0	0
0	0	1	1	0
0	1	0	1	0
0	1	1	0	1
1	0	0	1	0
1	0	1	0	1
1	1	0	0	1
1	1	1	1	1

Table 4.3 Addition of Two Bits

Bit 1	Bit 2	Sum	Carry
0	0	0	0
0	1	1	0
1	0	1	0
1	1	0	1

of bits. Thus when adding two binary numbers it is necessary to consider not only each pair of bits but also the carry digit from the previous pair.

Table 4.4 is a **truth table** which summarises all the possible combinations of two bits and a carry-in and the resulting sum and carry-out.

For example:

$$A = 10011010 = 154 \text{ (decimal)}$$
$$B = 01010111 = 87 \text{ (decimal)}$$

$$\text{Carry} = \underline{00111100}$$

$$A + B = \underline{11110001} = 241 \text{ (decimal)}$$

All Add instructions on the 8085 use either register, immediate or register indirect addressing and affect all the flag bits. Examples of each addressing mode are given below.

Register Addressing

Example: ADD   B

This results in the contents of the B-register being added to the current contents of the A-register. The result is placed in the A-register and the contents of the B-register are unchanged:

$$(A) \leftarrow (A) + (B)$$

After an ADD instruction the individual flag bits are affected as follows:

S   set if result is negative (i.e. m.s. bit of A is 1)
Z   set if result is zero (i.e. contents of A are all 0s)
AC set if carry generated from bit 3 (used with BCD arithmetic)
CY set if carry from bit 7 (i.e. m.s. bit)
P   reset

Immediate Addressing

Example: ADI   0F

This results in the immediate data 0F(hex) being added to the current contents of the A-register:

$$(A) \leftarrow (A) + 0F$$

All flags are affected.

Register Indirect Addressing

Example: ADD   M

This results in the contents of the memory location whose address is contained in the H and L registers being added to the current contents of the A-register. The result is placed in the A-register:

$$(A) \leftarrow (A) + ((H)(L))$$

All flags are affected.

4.3.2   Subtract Instructions

The subtraction of two binary numbers is similar to addition except that the carry is now replaced by a borrow. The subtraction of two bits is summarised in the truth table given in Table 4.5. Both bit 2

Table 4.5   Subtraction of Two Bits and a Borrow-in

Bit 1	Bit 2	Borrow-in	Difference	Borrow-out
0	0	0	0	0
0	0	1	1	1
0	1	0	1	1
0	1	1	0	1
1	0	0	1	0
1	0	1	0	0
1	1	0	0	0
1	1	1	1	1

and borrow-in are subtracted from bit 1 to produce the difference and, if necessary, a borrow-out. For example,

$$A = 10011011 = 155 \text{ (decimal)}$$

$$B = 01010111 = 87 \text{ (decimal)}$$

$$\text{Borrow} = \underline{10001000}$$

$$A - B \quad \underline{01000100} \quad = \quad 68 \text{ (decimal)}$$

The subtract instructions are identical to the above add instructions except that a subtraction operation is performed in place of the add operation. Again, all flags are affected. The corresponding subtraction instructions for each of the above addition examples are

SUB   B
SUI   0F
SUB   M

4.3.3   Increment Instructions

The increment instructions use either register or register indirect addressing to increment the contents of either a processor register or a memory location by unity. All flags *except* the carry flag are affected.

Register Addressing

Example: INR   A

results in the contents of the A-register being incremented by unity:

$$(A) \leftarrow (A) + 1$$

In addition to being able to increment the contents of a single register, a number of instructions are provided to increment the combined contents of a pair of registers.

For example: INX   H

This results in the combined contents of register pair H and L being incremented by unity:

$$(H)(L) \leftarrow (H)(L) + 1$$

This is particularly useful when accessing a series of values from memory.

Register Indirect Addressing

Example: INR   M

This results in the contents of the memory location whose address is contained in the H and L registers being incremented by unity:

$$((H)(L)) \leftarrow ((H)(L)) + 1$$

4.3.4   Decrement Instructions

These instructions are identical to the increment instructions except that the contents of either the processor register(s) or memory location is decremented by unity. The corresponding decrement instructions are

    DCR   A
    DCX   H
    DCR   M

Program Example 4.1:   Unsigned Arithmetic

The program example of Fig. 4.2 uses unsigned binary number representation. The two registers A and B are first loaded with immediate data and their contents are added together. A third number is then subtracted from the contents of A using immediate addressing and finally the new contents of A are decremented by unity.

As has been mentioned, the microprocessor is not aware of the type of number representation being used by the programmer; it simply performs the indicated arithmetic operation and it is the programmer who represents and interprets the binary patterns in the required way. This can be seen from the following example.

Assembly Instructions	*Action*
MVI A, 53	$(A) \leftarrow 53$ (hex) i.e. 83_{10}
MVI B, 3A	$(B) \leftarrow 3A$ (hex) i.e. 58_{10}
ADD B	$(A) \leftarrow (A) + (B)$ i.e. $(A) \leftarrow 141_{10}$
SBI 8C	$(A) \leftarrow (A) - 8C$ (hex) i.e. $(A) \leftarrow 1_{10}$
DCR A	$(A) \leftarrow (A) - 1$ i.e. $(A) \leftarrow 0$

Fig. 4.2   Program Example 4.1

Assembly Instructions	Action
MVI A, 23	(A) ← 23 (hex) i.e. $+35_{10}$
MVI B, B8	(B) ← B8 (hex) i.e. -72_{10}
ADD B	(A) ← (A) + (B) i.e. (A) ← -37_{10}
SBI DB	(A) ← (A) – DB (hex) i.e. (A) ← 0
DCR A	(A) ← (A) – 1 i.e. (A) ← –1

Fig. 4.3 Program Example 4.2

Program Example 4.2:   Signed Arithmetic

The program example of Fig. 4.3 is the same as Example 4.1 except that the initial numbers have been changed to represent a positive and a negative value and the final result is negative. Two's complement signed number representation is therefore used and particular care should be taken to interpret the signs of the numbers in the correct way.

4.4 Multiprecision Arithmetic Instructions

Although 8 bits are sufficient to represent a data value for many microprocessor applications, some necessitate the use of 16 or more bits. Most 8-bit microprocessors, therefore, provide a number of arithmetic instructions for manipulating numbers of more than 8 bits.

4.4.1   16-bit Arithmetic

In Chapter 3 it was mentioned that the 8085 provides some data transfer instructions for loading 16-bit (2 byte) immediate data into a register pair—BC, DE or HL. There are also instructions for incrementing and decrementing the combined 16-bit contents of a register pair and also for performing double length (16-bit) addition.

For example: INX   B

This results in the combined contents of registers B and C being incremented by unity. No flags are affected:

$$(B)(C) \leftarrow (B)(C) + 1$$

For example: DCX   D

This results in the combined contents of registers D and E being decremented by unity. No flags are affected:

$$(D)(E) \leftarrow (D)(E) - 1$$

For example: DAD   B

This results in the 16-bit contents of the register pair BC being added to the 16-bit contents of the register pair HL. The result is placed in the register pair HL. Only the carry flag is affected: it is set if there is a carry out from the most significant bit of H during the addition operation, otherwise it is reset:

$$(H)(L) \leftarrow (H)(L) + (B)(C)$$

4.4.2   Multiprecision Arithmetic; The Carry Flag

If more than 16-bit accuracy is required, there are no single instructions available for performing arithmetic operations and instead a number of instructions must be used. For example, consider the addition of two 24-bit (3 byte) numbers. Each number would require three memory locations and also the total addition operation would require three separate 8-bit additions as illustrated in Fig. 4.4.

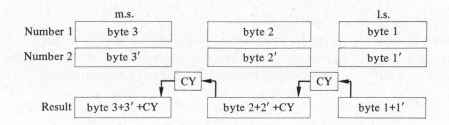

Fig. 4.4 Multiprecision arithmetic

Fig. 4.4 shows that it is also necessary to add the carry bit (CY) when adding together the second and third pair of bytes. The 8085, therefore, provides additional add and subtract instructions which use the carry (or borrow) bit.

For example: ADC   M

This results in the contents of the memory location whose address is contained in registers H and L *and* the contents of the CY flag being added to the contents of the A-register. The result is placed in the

A-register and all flags are affected:

$$(A) \leftarrow (A) + ((H)(L)) + (CY)$$

Another example: SBB   M

This is the same as the above except that a subtraction operation is performed:

$$(A) \leftarrow (A) - ((H)(L)) - (CY)$$

Program Example 4.3:   Multiprecision Arithmetic

The program example of Fig. 4.5 adds together the 24-bit (3 byte) number which is stored in the three consecutive memory locations starting at address 2080 to the 24-bit number which is stored in the three memory locations starting at address 2083. The 24-bit result replaces the first number.

Assembly Instructions	Comments
LXI H, 2083	Initialise IIL to contain 2083.
LDA 2080	
ADD M	Add 1st pair of bytes.
STA 2080	
INX H	Increment HL.
LDA 2081	
ADC M	Add 2nd pair of bytes together with carry.
STA 2081	
INX H	Increment HL.
LDA 2082	
ADC M	Add 3rd pair of bytes together with carry.
STA 2082	

Fig. 4.5   Program Example 4.3

4.5 BCD Arithmetic

It is advantageous in some microprocessor applications to represent numbers in binary coded decimal (BCD) form. Most microprocessors, therefore, provide an instruction which, together with the basic arithmetic instructions, allow binary coded decimal data to be manipulated.

Consider the addition of two 2-digit BCD numbers:

Example 1: Number 1   0110 0010 = 62 BCD
            Number 2   0010 0101 = 25 BCD

Normal binary sum = 1000 0111   (CY ← 0, AC ← 0)
Required BCD sum = 1000 0111 = 87 BCD

Example 2: Number 1   0111 1001 = 79 BCD
            Number 2   0001 0110 = 16 BCD

Normal binary sum = 1000 1111   (CY ← 0, AC ← 0)
Required BCD sum = 1001 0101 = 95 BCD

Example 3: Number 1   0011 1001 = 39 BCD
            Number 2   0100 1000 = 48 BCD

Normal binary sum = 1000 0001   (CY ← 0, AC ← 1)
Required BCD sum = 1000 0111 = 87 BCD

It can be deduced from these three examples that if the normal binary addition of each 4-bit group produces an answer which is less than 9 *and* no auxiliary carry (AC) is generated when adding the two least significant BCD digits, the result is correct. However, if the result of the addition is greater than 9, *or* an auxiliary carry is generated, a correction must be made. It can readily be shown that the required correction is the addition of +6 to the normal binary sum. Consider example 2 above:

Normal binary sum =   1000 1111   (CY ← 0, AC ← 0)
Add +6   = +0000 0110

Corrected BCD sum =   1001 0101 = 95 BCD

Similarly, in example 3 above, when adding the two least significant pair of BCD digits, an auxiliary carry is generated and consequently a similar correction must be made:

Normal binary sum =   1000 0001   (CY ← 0, AC ← 1)
Add +6   = + 0000 0110

Corrected BCD sum =   1000 0111 = 87 BCD

Thus the Intel 8085, for example, provides the following instruction which may be used to automatically adjust the result produced by a normal binary addition operation when BCD data is being manipulated:

DAA   (Decimal Adjust Accumulator)

This results in the 8-bit number in the A-register being adjusted to form two 4-bit BCD digits by the following process:

1 If the value of the l.s. 4 bits of the A-register is greater than 9 *or* if the AC flag is set, 6 is added to the A-register.
2 If the value of the m.s. 4 bits of the A-register is now greater than 9 *or* if the CY flag is set, 6 is added to the m.s. 4 bits of the A-register.

Since both halves of the A-register are corrected and also both the carry (CY) and auxiliary carry (AC) flags are affected, it is clearly possible to perform multiprecision BCD arithmetic using the same instruction. This is illustrated in the following example.

Program Example 4.4:   BCD Arithmetic

The program example of Fig. 4.6 adds together two 4-digit (16-bit) BCD numbers, and forms the corrected 4-digit BCD sum. The first number is stored in the two consecutive memory locations starting at address 2080 and the second is stored in the two locations starting at address 2082. The result replaces the first number.

A correction must also be made when performing subtraction of BCD numbers but it should be noted that this is different from the correction required for addition. The correction can readily be deduced from examples and is summarised in Fig. 4.7. The table of Fig. 4.7 shows the state of the carry flags and the contents of the A-register *after* the normal binary subtraction operation (SUB, SUI, DCR) has been performed.

Two example subtractions are now given to illustrate the corrections.

Example 1:   Number 1 =   0100 0111 = 47 BCD
              Number 2 =   0011 0010 = 32 BCD

Normal binary difference =   0001 0101   (CY ← 0, AC ← 0)
          Add 00   +0000 0000

Corrected BCD difference = 0001 0101 = 15 BCD

Example 2:   Number 1 =   1000 0001 = 81 BCD
              Number 2 =   0110 1001 = 69 BCD
Normal binary difference =   0001 1000   (CY ← 0, AC ← 1)
              Add FA   +1111 1010

Corrected BCD difference = 0001 0010 = 12 BCD

The decimal adjust instruction of some microprocessors – the Zilog Z80, for example – automatically performs the appropriate correction after an addition *and* a subtraction operation by remembering the type of arithmetic operation performed before the decimal adjust instruction is executed. In other microprocessors – the Intel 8085, for example – it is the responsibility of the programmer to determine and perform the appropriate correction operation when performing subtraction with BCD numbers.

4.6 Logical Operations

So far in this and the previous chapter it has been assumed that the data within the microcomputer is always representing a numerical value. In many applications, however, the data may simply be indicating the state of, say, a controlled system. For example, a single binary bit may indicate the state of a control valve: 0 = valve open, 1 = valve closed. Thus the 8-bit binary value 0110 0111 may mean control valves 1, 2, 3, 6 and 7 are closed whilst control valves 4, 5 and 8 are open. In addition to the arithmetic instructions already introduced, a microprocessor has available a number of data manipulation instructions which are primarily included to manipulate non-numeric data of this kind. These are the logical instructions and some examples are now considered.

4.6.1 Logical AND

The logical AND instructions perform the bit-by-bit AND operation between the contents of the A-register and either immediate data or the contents of another processor register or a memory location.

The truth table for the AND function is shown in Table 4.6. A typical application of this instruction is to test the state of a specific bit in a group of, say, 8 bits.

For example: ANI   40

This results in the bit-by-bit logical AND operation between the contents of the A-register and the immediate data 40(hex). The result is placed in the A-register:

(A) ← (A)   AND   40

Assembly Instructions	Comments
LXI H, 2082	Initialise HL to contain 2082.
LDA 2080	
ADD M	
DAA	Add 1st pair of bytes and form corrected sum.
STA 2080	
INX H	Increment HL.
LDA 2081	
ADC M	
DAA	Add 2nd pair of bytes and form corrected sum.
STA 2081	

Fig. 4.6 Program Example 4.4

Carry CY	Upper hex digit (bits 7-4)	Auxiliary carry AC	Lower hex digit (bits 3-0)	Correction to be added
0	0–9	0	0–9	00
0	0–8	1	6–F	FA
1	7–F	0	0–9	A0
1	6–F	1	6–F	9A

Fig. 4.7 BCD subtraction corrections

Table 4.6 AND Function Truth Table

Bit 1	Bit 2	Bit 1 AND Bit 2
0	0	0
0	1	0
1	0	0
1	1	1

For example:

$$(A) = 0110\ 0100$$
$$40 = \underline{0100\ 0000}$$

$$(A)\ AND\ 40 = \underline{0100\ 0000} \qquad P\ is\ reset\ (odd)$$

Thus if bit 7 of A was logical 1, the new contents of A are non-zero. Conversely, if bit 7 of A was logical 0, the new contents of A will be zero.

All logical instructions affect the parity flag P. If the number of 1s in the result (the new contents of the A-register) is *odd*, P is reset (0). If the number of 1s is *even*, P is set (1). Thus with the above example, P is reset.

4.6.2   Logical OR

The logical OR instructions are similar to the AND instructions except that the bit-by-bit OR operation is performed. The truth table for the OR function is given in Table 4.7.

For example: ORA   B

The contents of the A-register are OR-ed with the contents of the B-register. The result is placed in the A-register:

$$(A) \leftarrow (A)\ \ OR\ \ (B)$$

For example:

$$(A) = 0110\ 0100$$
$$(B) = \underline{1001\ 0101}$$

$$(A)\ OR\ (B) = \underline{1111\ 0101} \qquad P\ is\ set\ (even)$$

4.6.3   Exclusive-OR (XOR)

The exclusive-OR operation differs from the normal logical OR insomuch that with the former, when both bits are logical 1s, the result is 0. The truth table for the exclusive-OR function is given in Table 4.8. The range of exclusive-OR instructions provided are similar to the OR instructions and are used extensively, for example, in detecting and correcting errors that may occur when transmitting binary information.

For example: XRA   M

This results in the bit-by-bit exclusive-OR operation between the contents of the A-register and the contents of the memory location

Table 4.7 OR Function Truth Table		
Bit 1	Bit 2	Bit 1 OR Bit 2
0	0	0
0	1	1
1	0	1
1	1	1

Table 4.8 XOR Function Truth Table		
Bit 1	Bit 2	Bit 1 XOR Bit 2
0	0	0
0	1	1
1	0	1
1	1	0

whose address is contained in the H and L registers. The result is placed in the A-register:

$$(A) \leftarrow (A) \quad XOR \quad ((H)(L))$$

For example:

$$(A) = 1001\,1011$$
$$((H)(L)) = \underline{1100\,1101}$$

$$(A)\ XOR\ ((H)(L)) = \underline{0101\,0110} \qquad P \text{ is set (even)}$$

4.6.4 Rotate

The three previous instruction types – logical AND, OR and XOR – performed the bit-by-bit logical operation between two 8-bit patterns. In addition, the logical group contains instructions to rotate (shift) a binary value left or right one place. This is useful, for example, when performing binary multiplication and division: a left shift is a times 2 operation and a right shift is a divide by 2 operation.

For example: RLC

The contents of the A-register are rotated left one place. The least significant bit and the carry flag are both set to the value shifted out of the most significant bit position. This is shown in Fig. 4.8.

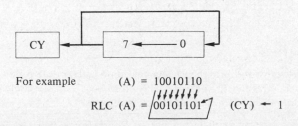

For example   (A) = 10010110

RLC (A) = 00101101   (CY) ← 1

Fig. 4.8 Rotate left

4.6.5   Compare

The compare instructions are often useful. They compare two values – the contents of the A-register and either immediate data or the contents of a processor register or memory location – without modifying either value. The result of the comparison affects the flags and, as the next chapter shows, these may be tested to determine the next operation to be performed.

For example: CMP   B

The contents of the B-register are compared with the contents of the A-register. The Z flag is set to 1 if the contents are equal; the CY flag is set to 1 if the contents of A are less than the contents of B.

Program Example 4.5:   Logical Operations

The program example given in Fig. 4.9 first loads immediate data into registers A and B and then performs a series of logical operations. First the contents of A and B are compared, the contents of A are then rotated left, the new contents of A are then AND-ed with a constant, and finally the resulting contents of A are OR-ed with the contents of B.

Assembly Instructions	*Action*
MVI A, F0	(A) ← F0 (hex)
MVI B, 0F	(B) ← 0F (hex)
CMP B	Z ← 0, CY ← 0
RLC	(A) ← E1, CY ← 1
ANI 81	(A) ← 81, CY ← 0, P ← 1
ORA B	(A) ← 8F, CY ← 0, P ← 0

Fig. 4.9   Program Example 4.5

Exercises

4.1   Derive the equivalent decimal numbers from the following 8-bit binary patterns interpreted in turn as unsigned binary, two's complement signed binary, and binary coded decimal representations:

0110	1001	0111	0110	1001	0011
0010	1000	1000	1000	1000	0111

4.2 Perform the following arithmetic operations using unsigned binary number representation:

$$103 + 27$$
$$67 + 118$$
$$105 - 94$$
$$56 - 19$$

4.3 Perform the following arithmetic operations using two's complement signed binary number representation:

$$-105 + 94$$
$$-56 + 19$$
$$103 - 27$$
$$67 - 118$$

4.4 Perform the following arithmetic operations using BCD number representation. First perform the normal binary addition/subtraction operation and then add the appropriate corrections derived in section 4.5:

$$34 + 52$$
$$19 + 27$$
$$75 - 42$$
$$81 - 39$$

4.5 Determine the number which is in the A-register after execution of each instruction in the following sequence:

```
MVI   A,  13
ADI   41
DAA
```

4.6 Write an assembly language program to perform the following arithmetic operation using two's complement signed binary number representation:

$$-56 + (-27)$$

4.7 Determine the result of performing the AND, OR and XOR logical operations on the following pairs of bytes:

```
AE,   14
2B,   8F
37,   48
A5,   5A
```

4.8 Determine the number which is in the A-register and the state of the carry and parity flags after execution of each instruction in the following sequence:

```
MVI   A,  9E
MVI   B,  A4
RLC
ANI   C2
ORA   B
```

5 Transfer of Control

5.1 Introduction

The previous two chapters have been concerned with program instructions from the data transfer and data manipulation groups. The flexibility and versatility of the stored program concept on which computers are based, however, results primarily from the computer's ability to transfer control, or branch, to an instruction that is not in sequential order. This is achieved with instructions from the transfer of control group. All these instructions act on the program counter and, as will be shown, it is possible to execute a block of instructions many times over with the number of times determined either by program data or the state of, say, a processor flag.

5.2 Jump Instructions

A **jump instruction** is used to break normal sequential execution and branch to a different part of the program. This is accomplished by loading the address of the next out-of-sequence instruction into the program counter, thus forcing the processor to fetch the contents of this new location for its next instruction. This new address is usually specified in the instruction. For example,

        JMP   20B3

which in 8085 machine code looks like Fig. 5.1.

Execution of this instruction causes an **unconditional** jump to memory location 20B3 for the next instruction. Thus if this instruction was stored in memory starting at address 2000, for example, after execution of the instruction the program counter, instead of containing 2003 (the start address of the next sequential instruction) would contain 20B3.

When writing a program in symbolic assembly language, the absolute address of the destination instruction is often not known until the program has been fully developed. It is for this reason that the label

Memory address	A	C3	JMP operation
	A+1	B3	l.s. byte of address
	A+2	20	m.s. byte of address

Fig. 5.1 Unconditional jump

Absolute Address	Instruction
–	–
–	–
2000	JMP LAB1
–	–
.	.
.	.
.	.
20B3	LAB1 : Destination Instruction

Fig. 5.2 Symbolic addressing

field is provided with an assembly language instruction. A label is used to indicate the destination address of a jump instruction and this is only translated into its absolute hexadecimal form during the assembly process. Thus the above instruction would take the form:

JMP   LAB1

where LAB1 is a label associated with the instruction stored at memory location 20B3. This is illustrated in Fig. 5.2.

5.2.1 Conditional Jump

The above instruction is known as an *unconditional* jump instruction since, when executed, a branch to the address contained within the instruction will always occur. The real flexibility of jump instructions, however, is derived from the **conditional jump instructions** since

Op-Code	Condition	Flag Status
JNZ	not zero	Z=0
JZ	zero	Z=1
JNC	no carry	C=0
JC	carry	C=1
JPO	parity odd	P=0
JPE	parity even	P=1
JP	plus	S=0
JM	minus	S=1

Fig. 5.3 Conditional jump instructions

these result in a branch for the next instruction *only* if a specified condition is satisfied, otherwise the next sequential instruction is executed.

The conditions which may be specified are determined by the state of the various flags in the processor flag register. The conditions which may be specified for the Intel 8085, for example, are shown in Fig. 5.3.

Thus a typical conditional jump instruction is

JNZ   LAB1

This is read as: jump if zero-flag not set to LAB1; and would result in the next instruction being fetched from the address associated with the label LAB1 *only* if the zero flag in the processor flag register was not set ($Z = 0$), otherwise the next sequential instruction will be fetched.

5.3 Flowcharts

Before any program involving branching can be written, it is necessary to plan the logical sequence of events to be carried out to achieve the desired goal. A number of techniques may be used, but the most useful for assembly language programs is the construction of a **flowchart**. This is simply a diagram which indicates the sequence of, and actions required in, a program and the points where branching is required.

The symbols used in a flowchart are perhaps best illustrated by means of examples.

Program Example 5.1: Flowcharts

Consider a simple program to add together the ten numbers 1–10. A flowchart for this program is shown in Fig. 5.4.

Let the C-register contain the number to be added to the running total and the B-register contain the running total.

The assembly language instructions given in Fig. 5.5 for the program have been evolved using the flowchart of Fig. 5.4. The CPI (compare immediate) and JNZ (jump not zero) instructions in Fig. 5.5 are used to determine when the count has reached 11. This combination is frequently used to provide a conditional transfer of control.

Program Example 5.2: Jump Instructions

A common requirement when a microcomputer is interfaced to other equipment is to compute a time delay in the program. A microcomputer-based road traffic light controller, for example, would need to compute a time delay to implement the sequencing of the light changes.

Since each machine instruction takes a specific amount of time to be executed (typically a few microseconds), it is possible to compute a time delay by executing a group of instructions a preset number of times. The delay obtained is then approximately proportional to the number of times this group of instructions (or loop) is executed. Let the desired delay and hence loop count be held in the C-register. A flowchart for this program is given in Fig. 5.6. This flowchart can now be readily translated into the assembly language program of Fig. 5.7.

The basic time delay is derived from the six no-operation instructions (NOP). These instructions do not affect any of the processor registers or memory and the delay can be readily extended by substituting them with different instructions. Note that the compare and conditional jump instructions are again used to determine the transfer of control.

5.4 Subroutines Frequently within a program it may be necessary to perform a particular sub-task many times over. It is highly desirable not to have to repeat the section of machine code each time the sub-task is required. It is therefore necessary to be able to transfer control in a program to a section of often-used code or **subroutine** designed to perform the sub-task and then return control to the main instruction sequence.

Assembly Instructions	Comments
MVI B, 00	Initialise running total.
MVI C, 01	Initialise number count.
LAB1: MOV A, B	Bring running total to A.
ADD C	Add number count.
MOV B, A	Restore running total in B.
INR C	Increment count.
MOV A, C	Bring count to A.
CPI 0B	Has count reached 11?
JNZ LAB1	No – Jump back to LAB1.
————	Yes – end; total in B.

Fig. 5.5 Assembly for Program Example 5.1

```
BEGIN
  │
  ▼
┌─────────────────────────┐
│ Initialise running total│
│ to 0 and number count   │
│ to 1.                   │
└─────────────────────────┘
  │
  ▼
┌─────────────────────────┐
│ Add number count to     │
│ running total.          │
│ Increment count by 1.   │
└─────────────────────────┘
  │
  ▼
  ╱───────────╲
 ╱ Is count    ╲
 ╲ less than or ╱
  ╲ equal to 10?╱
   ╲──────────╱
  yes │ no
      ▼
    END
```

Fig. 5.4 Flowchart for Program Example 5.1

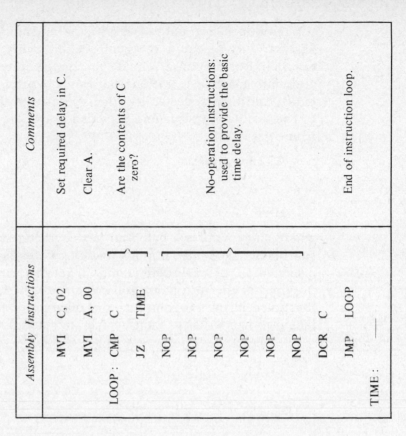

Assembly Instructions	Comments
MVI C, 02	Set required delay in C.
MVI A, 00	Clear A.
LOOP : CMP C	Are the contents of C zero?
JZ TIME	
NOP	No-operation instructions: used to provide the basic time delay.
NOP	
NOP	
NOP	
NOP	
NOP	
DCR C	
JMP LOOP	
TIME : ——	End of instruction loop.

Fig. 5.7 Assembly for Program Example 5.2

BEGIN

Load desired delay time parameter into C.

Are the contents of C-register zero? yes

no

Execute delay instructions. Decrement C-register.

END

Fig. 5.6 Flowchart for Program Example 5.2

Subroutines not only save program memory because it is not necessary to repeat a program section every time a sub-task is required, but they also provide the opportunity to structure a program into convenient sections that can be written and tested independently and then collected together to perform the overall task.

The two basic instructions provided to call a subroutine and return from it are

CALL   nnnn

and

RET

where nnnn is the two-byte four hex character starting address of the subroutine. The RETurn instruction is the last instruction to be executed in the subroutine and it returns control to the calling program at the instruction following the CALL instruction. This is illustrated in the program memory diagram of Fig. 5.8. In assembly language it is usual to indicate the start address of a subroutine by

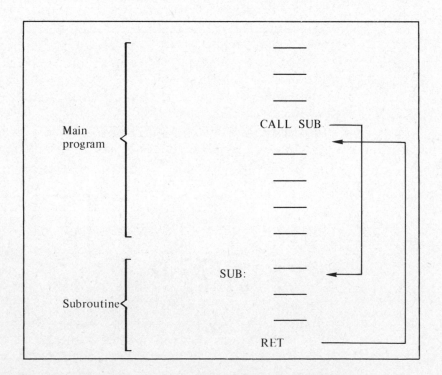

Fig. 5.8 Memory diagram illustrating a subroutine CALL

means of a label (symbolic name) and this is only translated into the corresponding four hex character absolute address during the assembly process.

When the microprocessor executes a subroutine CALL instruction, in addition to transferring control to the start address of the subroutine, it must also remember the current address within the main program so that it can return control to that point when the RET instruction is executed. This is accomplished by saving the current contents of the program counter register (PC) on a stack.

A **stack** is simply a last-in first-out queue which is implemented as a set of successive locations either within the processor itself or, more usually, in the system memory. The stack pointer register (SP) within the processor always points to the address which currently holds the entry at the top of the stack, and consequently its contents change as each subroutine call and return instruction is executed. If the stack is implemented in the system memory as on the Intel 8085, the initial content of the stack pointer is arbitrary and it is usually initialised to point to an unused area of memory.

The sequence of operations and the appropriate contents of the stack pointer and program counter during a subroutine call are illustrated in Fig. 5.9. It is assumed that the stack pointer (SP) currently contains 20C2 and, as is shown, its contents are *decremented* by two as the contents of the program counter (PC) – two bytes – are saved when the subroutine call is executed.

Whenever a RETurn instruction is executed, the process illustrated is reversed. The program counter is loaded (least significant byte first) with the contents at the top of the stack, the stack pointer is *incremented* twice, and control returns to the instruction following the subroutine call. Subroutine call and return instructions are available that are conditional in just the same way and for the same range of conditions as conditional jump instructions.

Program Example 5.3: Subroutines

The previous program example was a short program to compute a time delay. This can conveniently be made into a subroutine by placing a RET instruction with the label TIME at the end of the program. In order to make this subroutine useful for other parts of an imaginary application program, it is desirable to set the delay time in the main program and not in the subroutine itself. In this way the same subroutine can implement a variety of delay times. To implement this, the C-register is used to pass the required time delay parameter to the subroutine (TIMDLY). This is shown in Fig. 5.10.

Memory Address		Contents	Symbolic Instruction
	.		
	.		
	.		
	2010	CD	
Main Program	2011	48	CALL SUB PC = 2013
	2012	20	
	.		
	.		
	2048	XX	SUB : Subroutine
Subroutine	2049	XX	Instructions
	.		
	.		
	.		
	20C0	XX	
Stack	20C1	XX	SP = 20C2
	20C2		

(i)   CALL instruction brought from memory – PC incremented

Memory Address		Contents	Symbolic Instructions
	.		
	.		
	.		
	2010	CD	
Main Program	2011	48	CALL SUB PC = 2048
	2012	20	
	.		
	.		
	2048	XX	SUB: –
Subroutine	2049	XX	–
	.		
	.		
	.		
	20C0	13	
Stack	20C1	20	SP = 20C0
	20C2	XX	

(ii)   PC contents saved and contents of SP decremented

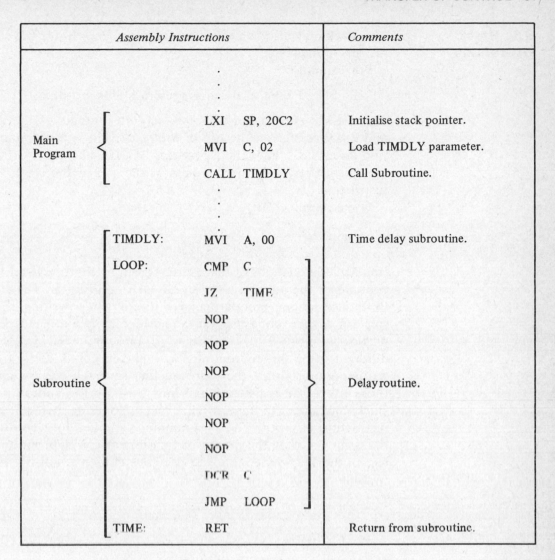

Assembly Instructions			Comments
		.	
		.	
		.	
Main Program	LXI	SP, 20C2	Initialise stack pointer.
	MVI	C, 02	Load TIMDLY parameter.
	CALL	TIMDLY	Call Subroutine.
		.	
		.	
		.	
TIMDLY:	MVI	A, 00	Time delay subroutine.
LOOP:	CMP	C	
	JZ	TIME	
	NOP		
	NOP		
	NOP		
Subroutine	NOP		Delay routine.
	NOP		
	NOP		
	DCR	C	
	JMP	LOOP	
TIME:	RET		Return from subroutine.

Fig. 5.10 Assembly for Program Example 5.3

Fig. 5.9 Subroutine CALL implementation (*opposite*)

5.5 Stack Operations

The stack may also be used as a temporary deposit for the contents of processor registers.

For example:

PUSH   PSW   (Push processor status word)

This pushes (saves) the combined 16-bit contents of the A-register and flags register on the top of the stack. There is a similar instruction for each of the pairs of registers BC, DE and HL. A register pair may be loaded with the contents of the top of the stack by a POP instruction.

For example:

POP   BC

transfers the contents of the address given by SP to register C and the contents of the address given by SP + 1 to register B. The PUSH and POP instructions are particularly useful when writing subroutines since, if a subroutine uses, say, registers A, B and C to perform its particular sub-task, the contents of these registers will be clearly different after the subroutine has been executed. It is usual when writing a subroutine, therefore, to first save the current contents of those processor registers which are used by the subroutine on the stack and then to restore the saved contents before the return instruction is given. The programmer can therefore continue using the contents of all the processor registers after a subroutine has been run in the knowledge that the previous contents will not have been corrupted.

5.6 Parameter Passing

The loop count used in the delay subroutine in program example 5.3 is known as a **parameter** (or argument) of the subroutine. In general, parameters may be required to pass data both to the subroutine for processing and also for passing results back from the subroutine to the calling program after processing. The mechanism used in the example was by means of one of the processor registers (the C-register) but a more flexible solution for passing parameters to and from a subroutine is by means of a pointer to the start address in the system memory where the parameters are stored. With the Intel 8085, this is usually accomplished by means of the HL register pair.

Program Example 5.4:   Parameter Passing

Program example 5.3 has been rewritten in Fig. 5.11 to illustrate the use of the HL register pair for passing the delay parameter and the use of the stack for saving the contents of those processor registers which are used by the subroutine during execution. The memory location used to store the delay parameter is 2080.

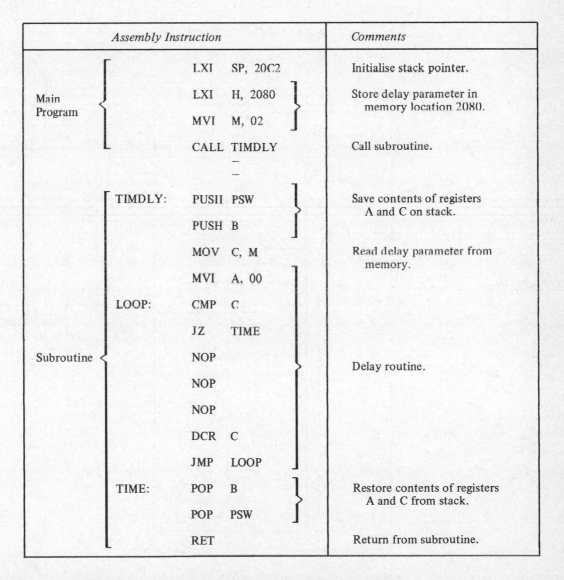

Assembly Instruction			Comments
Main Program	LXI	SP, 20C2	Initialise stack pointer.
	LXI	H, 2080	Store delay parameter in memory location 2080.
	MVI	M, 02	
	CALL	TIMDLY	Call subroutine.
TIMDLY:	PUSH	PSW	Save contents of registers A and C on stack.
	PUSH	B	
	MOV	C, M	Read delay parameter from memory.
	MVI	A, 00	
LOOP:	CMP	C	
	JZ	TIME	
Subroutine	NOP		Delay routine.
	NOP		
	NOP		
	DCR	C	
	JMP	LOOP	
TIME:	POP	B	Restore contents of registers A and C from stack.
	POP	PSW	
	RET		Return from subroutine.

Fig. 5.11 Parameter passing program (Example 5.4)

**5.7   Nested
Subroutines**

It is quite in order for a subroutine to call another subroutine within itself and indeed for that to call another. The last-in first-out stack mechanism always ensures that the correct return address is at the top of the stack when the RET instructions are encountered. Subroutines may be **nested** in this way to a depth determined only by the available read/write memory provided for the stack. This is illustrated in Fig. 5.12.

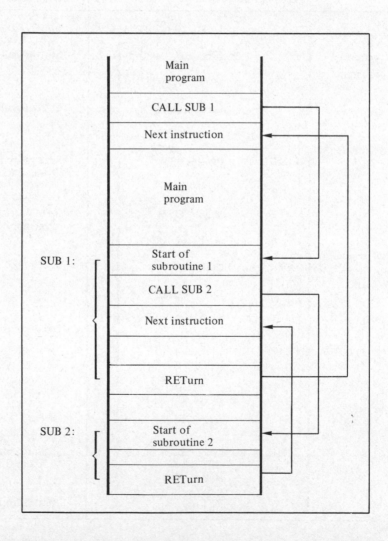

Fig. 5.12   Nested subroutines

Assembly Instruction		Comments
	—	
	—	
	LXI SP, 20C2	Initialise stack pointer.
Main Program	LXI H, 2080	Store delay parameter in memory location 2080.
	MVI M, FF	
	CALL TIMDLY1	Call subroutine 1.
	—	
	—	
	—	
TIMDLY1:	PUSH PSW	Save contents of registers A and C.
	PUSH B	
	MOV C, M	Read delay parameter from memory.
	MVI A, 00	
LOOP:	CMP C	
Subroutine 1	JZ TIME	
	LXI H, 2081	Store delay parameter in memory location 2081.
	MVI M, FF	
	CALL TIMDLY2	Call subroutine 2.
	DCR C	
	JMP LOOP	
TIME:	POP B	
	POP PSW	
	RET	
TIMDLY2:	PUSH PSW	As for TIMDLY1 except NOP instructions replace Subroutine Call.
Subroutine 2	—	
	—	
	—	
	RET	

Fig. 5.13   Assembly for Program Example 5.5

Program Example 5.5:   Nested Subroutines

The maximum time delay produced by the subroutine in the previous example can be greatly extended by making the basic delay instructions require more time to be executed. A convenient way of doing this is to replace the NOP instructions with a call to another similar delay subroutine. This is illustrated in Fig. 5.13.

Exercises

5.1 Find the final contents of the A-register after the following assembly language progam has been run:

```
        MVI   A, FF
LAB1:   DCR   A
        JNZ   LABI
        HALT
```

5.2 Determine the number of instructions executed in the following assembly language program:

```
        MVI   A, 00
LAB2:   INR   A
        JNZ   LAB2
        HALT
```

5.3 Design a flowchart and write an assembly language program to sum together the even numbers from 0 to 20.

5.4 Modify the program in Example 5.1 to form a subroutine. Transfer the number count to the subroutine as a parameter.

5.5 Design a flowchart and write an assembly language program for a subroutine to compute a time delay by incrementing the contents of the A-register by unity until a limit is reached which is passed to the subroutine as a parameter.

5.6 Modify the program in Example 5.5 to incorporate the above subroutine in place of TIMDLY2.

5.7 Assuming each program instruction is executed in 2 μs, estimate the maximum time delay that can be generated by program Example 5.5.

6 Digital Input and Output

6.1 Introduction

A microcomputer is basically a digital component that can examine digital input signals and perform functions as a consequence of these inputs to yield digital output signals. Since the external devices outside the microcomputer produce or accept signals which are not necessarily digital in nature, special interface circuitry is often required to transform these external signals into a form suitable for the microcomputer. This chapter is concerned with the basic mechanisms used in a microprocessor system to read digital inputs and produce digital outputs. The following two chapters describe some of the additional circuitry and control mechanisms which are required to **interface** the microcomputer to specific external input and output signals.

6.2 Digital Input and Output

A simple digital input to a microcomputer can be produced by a single pole **switch**. Fig. 6.1 shows how a logical 0 or 1 voltage level can be presented to the microcomputer depending on the switch position.

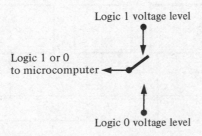

Logic 1 voltage level

Logic 1 or 0
to microcomputer

Logic 0 voltage level

Fig. 6.1 Logical input

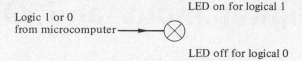

Fig. 6.2   A simple logical circuit

Similarly, a simple logical output from a microcomputer can be displayed using a **light-emitting diode** (LED) as illustrated in Fig. 6.2.

An LED indicator or a switch cannot be connected directly to the microcomputer bus, however, since the bus is used by the microprocessor to communicate with all the devices in the system. The information on the bus is therefore continuously changing as instructions are fetched from memory and executed. Information intended for an output indicator must therefore be **latched** by a suitable circuit. The processor can then send data to the output latching device which captures the data at the appropriate time determined by bus control signals and then provides a continuous output until new data is sent to it. Similarly, an input from a switch must be isolated from the data bus until the microprocessor is ready to read its logical value.

Considerable flexibility is available if a system incorporates a programmable input/output (PI/O) device to provide the necessary latching and isolation. These devices are usually organised into **ports** or groups of inputs and outputs, often of 8 bits. Each port can usually be programmed to be an input port or an output port or sometimes a mixture of inputs and outputs. A schematic diagram of a basic microcomputer incorporating a PI/O is shown in Fig. 6.3.

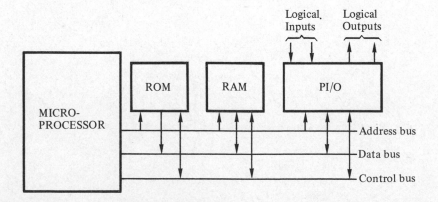

Fig. 6.3   A basic microcomputer

6.3 Memory Mapped Input/Output

A typical microcomputer system may contain a number of input/output devices all connected to the same bus. It is therefore necessary for each device to be separately addressed by the microprocessor.

There are basically two approaches to organising the addressing associated with the transfer of input/output data between a microcomputer bus and an input/output device: memory mapped input/output and programmed input/output. With **memory mapped input/output**, the available memory address space of the microcomputer is partitioned into two areas. One is a range of addresses associated with actual system memory (ROM and RAM), the other area is reserved for input/output devices. A typical memory map illustrating this approach is shown in Fig. 6.4.

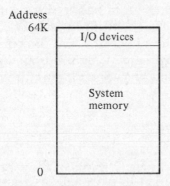

Fig. 6.4 Memory mapped input/output

Each input or output operation with this method is similar to a normal memory access and indeed the same instructions are used for both memory and input/output data transfers. The appropriate address is output on the address bus and recognised either by a memory device (ROM and RAM) or an input/output device (PI/O) or port, and the appropriate data is transferred on the data bus. This approach therefore has the advantage of having all the addressing modes used for memory access available for input/output data transfers. The major disadvantage is that the range of addresses available for memory is restricted.

6.4 Programmed Input/Output

The alternative approach is **programmed input/output** (or input/output mapped input/output). With this method, input/output data transfers are accomplished by means of special instructions executed by the processor – IN and OUT for the Intel 8085. The

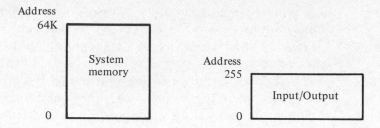

Fig. 6.5   Programmed input/output

microprocessor generates an input/output request signal to inform input/output devices (and memory) that the address on the address bus is for an input/output device. This provision means that no system memory space has to be reserved for input/output devices.

A typical scheme is illustrated in Fig. 6.5.

Note that although the Intel 8085 has, in common with most types of microprocessor, programmed input/output instructions, it is also possible to design a memory mapped input/output scheme around the microcomputer bus.

6.5 Programmable Input/Output Devices

Digital input and output in most microprocessors is controlled by programmable input/output devices and programmed input/output is normally used. A PI/O device can control a number of individual input and output lines. These are normally grouped into a number of ports, each comprised of eight lines which may be programmed to operate either as inputs or as outputs.

Before data may be read from or written to a port, it is necessary first to program the device into the configuration intended for the application. This is achieved by writing appropriate command information into a specific addressable register(s) within the device when the system is being initialised. After receiving this information, the device will then respond to further commands – either from the external circuitry or from the microprocessor itself – in the specified way. This is discussed further in section 6.5.2.

6.5.1   Handshake Control

For some applications it is necessary to synchronise the transfer of data between the PI/O and an external device and consequently most

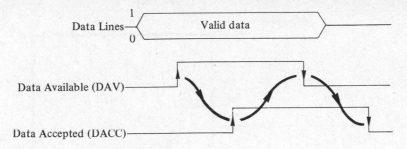

Fig. 6.6 Handshake control

PI/Os provide control lines for this function. Synchronisation is usually accomplished by means of a **handshake** procedure and a typical transfer sequence is illustrated in Fig. 6.6.

The data is first placed on the data lines by the sending device and the "data available" (DAV) line is set. The receiving device detects the setting of the DAV line, accepts the data, and then responds by setting the "data accepted" (DACC) line. The sending device interprets the setting of the DACC line as an acknowledgement of receipt of the data by the receiver and therefore resets the DAV line. Finally the receiver detects that the DAV line has been reset and in turn resets the DACC line to permit a further data transfer. These features are shown in the schematic diagram of a PI/O in Fig. 6.7.

There is a chip enable input on all the devices which are connected to the microprocessor bus – RAMs, ROMs, PI/Os – and they are used (in conjunction with the system address map) to ensure that only one device responds to each data transfer on the bus. Thus, whenever an address is present on the address bus of the microprocessor which is intended for the PI/O – usually determined by the presence of a logic 1 in a particular address bit position – this is detected and is used to drive the chip enable input line. Two additional address bits – usually the least significant pair – are then used to select the appropriate register within the PI/O itself – command, port A or port B. The appropriate input or output operation is then determined by the read and write lines respectively.

6.5.2 Port Initialisation

In some microprocessor systems each programmable input/output device is a separate integrated circuit but in others it is incorporated into other system components – processor or memory. In a typical Intel 8085 system, for example, three input/output ports are incorporated into each RAM memory circuit together with a timer device

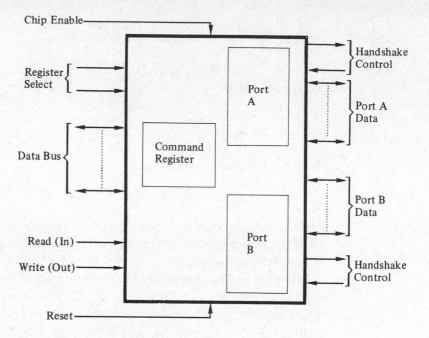

Fig. 6.7 A programmable input/output (PI/O)

(Intel 8155). Conceptually, however, the input/output ports and the timer are quite separate from the RAM memory and can therefore be considered independently.

The additional port of the Intel 8155 (port C) is only 6 bits and may be used either as a third input/output port or to provide control signals for ports A and B – for example, handshake control or interrupt control. The latter is described in the next chapter.

The command information required to initialise the ports in the Intel 8155 is a single 8-bit byte in which each bit is assigned some command significance as shown in Fig. 6.8. This command byte indicates that the timer and the input/output ports are programmed together. The command byte is transferred to the Intel 8155 using a specific address and the programmed output instruction, OUT. Thus, the instruction

   OUT   address

transfers the contents of the processor A-register to the addressed input/output device.

For example, if after deciding the system address map the PI/O is to respond to addresses starting with 20 (hex) on the least significant

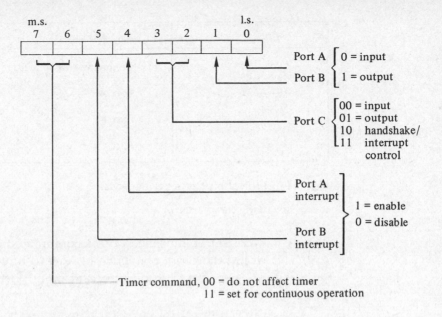

Fig. 6.8 The 8155 command byte

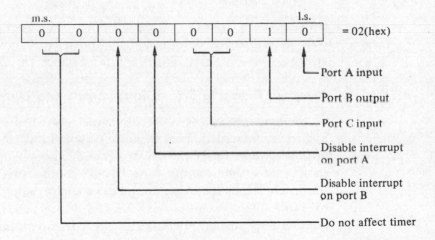

Fig. 6.9 Example command data

eight lines of the address bus, the instruction sequence:

MVI   A,   02

OUT   20

transfers command data 02(hex) to the command register in the

Address (hex)	Port/Register
20	Command/Status register
21	Port A
22	Port B
23	Port C

Fig. 6.10   Typical port/register addressing

selected 8155. The significance of this command data is shown in Fig. 6.9. This would therefore configure port A to be 8 inputs, port B to be 8 outputs and port C to be a second input port. The timer would not be affected.

Data is then transferred between the processor and these ports by using an IN or OUT instruction with a specific address for each port. Thus the instruction:

IN   address

transfers data from the addressed port to the A-register. The specific port or register is determined by the least significant 8-bits of the address bus. Fig. 6.10 shows a typical range of addresses.

Program Example 6.1:   Digital Input and Output

In the example of Fig. 6.11 the same address assignments as above have been assumed. Port A is first configured as an input port and port B as an output port. Data is then input from port A and the same data is then output to port B. This process is repeated continuously. Hence if, for example, a set of eight switches were connected to port A and a set of 8 LEDs to port B, the LEDs would continuously display the state of the corresponding eight switches.

Program Example 6.2:   Digital Output

As an additional example the program given in Fig. 6.12 initialises ports A, B and C as output ports and then outputs the decimal number 24937 in BCD form. The three ports are used as follows:

Port A	Port B	Port C
0010 0100	1001 0011	xxxx 0111
2 4	9 3	7

Assembly Instructions		Comments
	MVI A, 02	Load command byte in A.
	OUT 20	Load command register.
START:	IN 21	Read data from port A.
	OUT 22	Output data to port B.
	JMP START	Repeat.

Fig. 6.11 Program Example 6.1

Assembly Instructions		Comments
MVI A, 07		Load command byte in A.
OUT 20		Load command register.
MVI A, 24	}	Output 24 to port A.
OUT 21		
MVI A, 93	}	Output 93 to port B.
OUT 22		
MVI A, 07	}	Output 07 to port C.
OUT 23		

Fig. 6.12 Program Example 6.2

Program Example 6.3: Handshake Control

This program example is intended to illustrate how digital output (and input) can be controlled by a handshake procedure. This is particularly useful, for example, when the receiving device cannot accept data at the same rate at which the microcomputer can produce it or, conversely, if new data is produced by a device at a rate lower than the rate the microcomputer can absorb it.

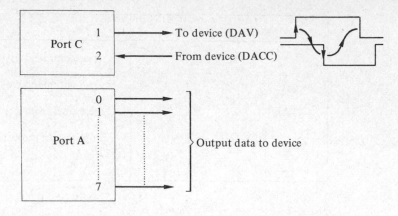

Fig. 6.13 Handshake example

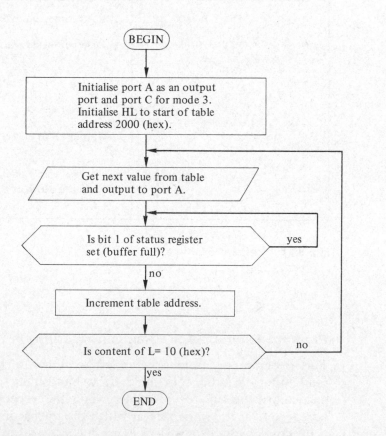

Fig. 6.14 Handshake control flowchart

The program uses the handshake control lines of port C to output 16 values from a table in memory – starting at address 2000(hex) – to an external device connected to port A. Fig. 6.13 is a schematic diagram of the arrangement.

Assuming port C has been initialised to operate in mode 3 (handshake mode), after data has been output to port A, bit 1 of port C will automatically go to logic 1, indicating to the external device that new data is available (DAV). The device will then respond by setting bit 2 of port C to logic 0 (DACC), indicating that it has read the data which is currently output on port A. Note that for the Intel 8155 this DACC signal is active low (i.e. logic 0 indicates data accepted).

Since the microprocessor must not output a new value to port A until the previous value has been read, the program must perform a loop waiting for the DACC signal to be received. The 8155, therefore, contains a separate status register which contains a number of status bits associated with port A and B data transfers. For instance,

Assembly Instructions	Comments
MVI A, 05	Initialise port A = output
OUT 20	port B = mode 3
LXI H, 2000	Initialise table pointer address.
NEXT: MOV A, M	Get next value and output to port A.
OUT 21	
LOOP: IN 20	Loop if bit 1 of status register is logic 1.
ANI 02	
JNZ LOOP	
INX H	Increment table address.
MOV A, L	All values output?
CPI 10	
JNZ NEXT	No: repeat.
HLT	Yes: end.

Fig. 6.15 Handshake control program

bit 1 of this register is set whenever data is output to port A – output buffer full – and this is only reset when the DACC input strobe for port A goes low.

Thus, after the microprocessor outputs a data value to port A, the program must loop until bit 1 of the status register goes to logic 0 again before outputting a new value. The required status word for the PI/O (address 20(hex)) is

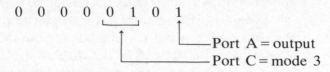

It should be noted that the contents of the status register are also examined using address 20(hex). A flowchart for the program is shown in Fig. 6.14 and an associated program listing in Fig. 6.15.

Exercises

6.1 Write an assembly language program to initialise ports A, B and C as input ports and read a data byte from each port.

6.2 Write an assembly language program to first initialise port A as an input port and port B as an output port, and then to input data from port A, complement the data and output the result to port B.

6.3 Write an assembly language program to initialise ports A and C as input ports and port B as an output port. The program should then input the data on ports A and C, sum the values together and output the result to port B.

7 Analogue Input/Output and Interrupts

7.1 Introduction

The previous chapter was concerned with the transfer of digital data between the microprocessor and an input or output (*peripheral*) device. In many microprocessor applications, however, the input data to be processed is a continuously varying analogue signal – for example the output voltage from a temperature transducer. Similarly, the output data from the microprocessor is often required in analogue form – for example a voltage to drive a motor. It is necessary therefore in these circumstances to have additional *interface* circuitry between the input/output ports of the microprocessor and the controlled peripheral devices, both to convert analogue signals into digital form and vice versa. A circuit that converts a digital signal into an equivalent analogue form is known as a **digital-to-analogue converter** (DAC) and the circuit that converts an analogue signal into a digital form is an **analogue-to-digital converter** (ADC). This chapter first describes the theory and operation of typical DACs and ADCs and then considers the interrupt facility provided by microprocessors for controlling input/output data transfers.

7.2 Digital-to-Analogue Conversion

A digital number can be converted to an analogue voltage by selectively adding voltages which are proportional to the weighting of each binary digit. This is done by means of a resistive ladder network and, as an example, Fig. 7.1 shows a 3-bit converter.

The three inputs A, B and C are each connected to either 0 volts or V volts depending on the digital output from the microprocessor – a logic 1 corresponds to V volts and a logic 0 to 0 volts. The accompanying truth table (Table 7.1) illustrates that the analogue output voltage increases in steps – determined by the number of binary digits – equivalent to the magnitude of the binary output.

Table 7.1

A	B	C	V_A
0	0	0	0
0	0	1	V/8
0	1	0	V/4
0	1	1	3V/8
1	0	0	V/2
1	0	1	5V/8
1	1	0	3V/4
1	1	1	7V/8

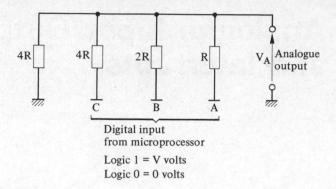

Digital input
from microprocessor

Logic 1 = V volts
Logic 0 = 0 volts

Fig. 7.1 Digital-to-analogue converter: outline operation

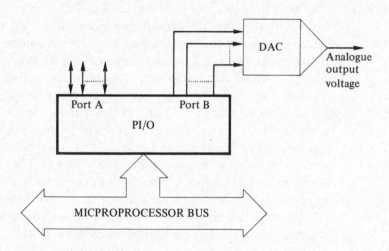

Fig. 7.2 A DAC driven from a PI/O port

Converters for eight or more bits are available in integrated circuit form. These are often based on a R-2R ladder network to produce binary weighted voltage increments, and they may be connected directly to the output port of a PI/O device. A schematic diagram of such an arrangement is shown in Fig. 7.2.

Program Example 7.1: Digital-to-Analogue Conversion

The program of Fig. 7.3 illustrates the DAC process by generating a sawtooth waveform. It is assumed that an 8-bit DAC is connected to port B of a PI/O which is in turn addressed as 22 (hex) [see Fig. 6.10,

Assembly Instructions			Comments
	MVI	A, 02	Initialise port B as an output port.
	OUT	20	
	MVI	A, 00	Set contents of A to zero.
COUNT:	OUT	22	Output current count.
	INR	A	Increment count.
	JMP	COUNT	Loop back.

Fig. 7.3 Program Example 7.1

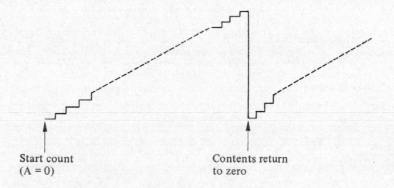

Start count
(A = 0)

Contents return
to zero

Fig. 7.4 Sawtooth waveform

p. 74]. A sawtooth waveform is then readily generated by using the A-register as a counter and outputting its contents after each increment. When the contents overflow and return to zero, the process repeats itself, as shown in Fig. 7.4.

7.3 Analogue-to-Digital Conversion

The conversion of an analogue signal to a digital number implies a process of signal sampling. A digital number can only accurately represent a changing analogue signal for a short period of time. However, the conversion process may take a relatively long time. The resulting sampling process is illustrated in Fig. 7.5.

7.3.1 The Shannon Sampling Theorem

It is possible to severely distort the digital representation of an

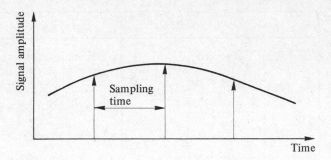

Fig. 7.5 Signal sampling; binary value represents signal only at indicated times

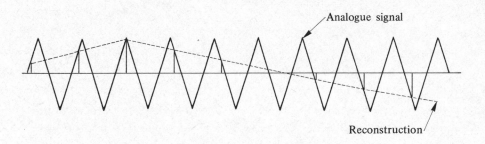

Fig. 7.6 Distortion due to under-sampling

analogue signal by sampling it too infrequently. The effect of under-sampling is shown in Fig. 7.6.

The Shannon sampling theorem provides that an analogue signal can be *completely* reconstructed if it is sampled at a uniform rate greater than twice the highest frequency component of the original signal. It is usual to sample a signal much more frequently than this theoretical minimum.

Fig. 7.6 shows a reconstructed signal which clearly has frequency components not present in the original signal due to under-sampling; this process is called **aliasing**. Care must be taken to ensure that system performance will not be impaired by this type of distortion, when performing analogue-to-digital conversion.

7.3.2 A Counter-based ADC

An analogue-to-digital converter employs a digital-to-analogue converter in a feedback loop. One common and inexpensive scheme is shown in Fig. 7.7.

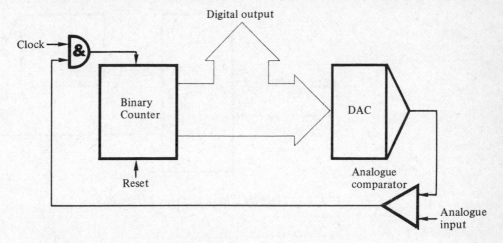

Fig. 7.7 A counter-based ADC

The sequence of operation is as follows. The counter is initially reset at the start of a conversion. Counter clock pulses are then enabled until the DAC output just exceeds the analogue input, causing the comparator to inhibit further counter clock pulses. The digital representation of the analogue input is then the binary number output of the counter.

During conversion the DAC output follows a stepped ramp (similar to that of Fig. 7.4) until it reaches a value approximately equal to the analogue input of the circuit. This type of conversion is slow since the DAC has to be allowed to settle after each clock; typically conversion times are around 1 millisecond. Even slower, but necessarily so, are ADCs based on the dual-ramp technique often used in digital voltmeters. This type of converter has useful "noise" rejection properties if the slow conversion time (20–200 milliseconds) can be tolerated.

7.3.3 Successive Approximation ADC

This type of converter is widely used when fast conversion is required. The basic technique is one of successively approximating a value for the digital output, altering this value each time in such a way as to approach the correct output.

Converters are widely available that employ hardware to implement this successive approximation algorithm (conversion times range from submicroseconds to 200 microseconds). It is possible, however, to use a microcomputer program to implement this al-

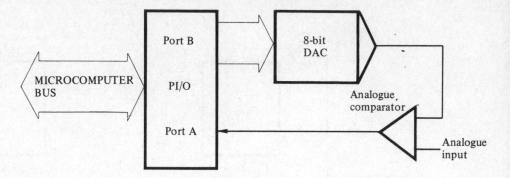

Fig. 7.8 Hardware for a software-based ADC

gorithm and implement analogue-to-digital conversion using a digital-to-analogue converter and a comparator. This approach is worth examining both to gain an understanding of the successive approximation technique and as an exercise in appreciating the hardware-software trade-offs that are possible in a microcomputer system. An outline of the hardware for an 8-bit converter is shown in Fig. 7.8.

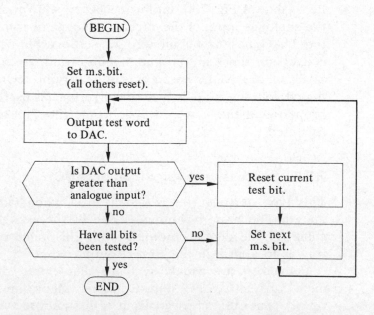

Fig. 7.9 Successive approximation flowchart

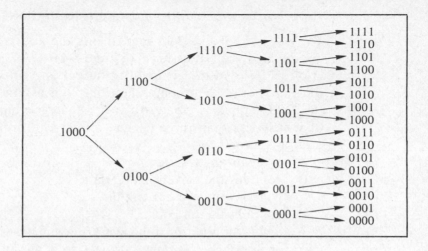

Fig. 7.10 4-bit approximation sequence

Upward decision if DAC output not greater than input.

Downward decision if DAC output greater than input.

The algorithm consists essentially of setting first the most significant bit of the DAC input to 1 and then successive bits in order of significance. At each step the comparator output is examined to see if the resulting DAC output is greater than or less than the analogue input. If it is greater, the current bit that is being tested is reset and the next most significant bit tested. If it is less, the bit being tested is held at 1 and the next bit is tested. The process repeats until all bits have been tested. A flowchart for the algorithm is shown in Fig. 7.9 and the approximation sequence for a 4-bit converter is given in Fig. 7.10.

An alternative statement of the algorithm is given below simply to illustrate a possible alternative representation of an algorithm.

Successive Approximation Algorithm
Start with m.s.b. of DAC set to 1, all other bits 0.

REPEAT
    Output DAC data.
    Read comparator output.
    IF   DAC output is greater than analogue input
        THEN reset current DAC test bit.
    Set next most significant bit of DAC data.
UNTIL all DAC data bits have been tested.

Current DAC data is digital equivalent of analogue input voltage.

Program Example 7.2:   Analogue-to-Digital Conversion

The program of Fig. 7.11 implements the above successive approximation algorithm. It assumes that the 8-bit DAC is connected to port B of a PI/O and the comparator output is connected to the m.s. bit (bit 7) of port A. The comparator output is assumed high (logical 1) if the DAC output is greater than the analogue input and low (logical 0) if it is less than the analogue input. The processor registers are used as follows:

A   is a working register
B   contains the current DAC data
C   contains the present test bit
D   contains the bit count.

A number of additional devices are available which are frequently used for interfacing analogue devices to a microcomputer. Three of these devices are mentioned below.

1   *Sample and hold circuits.* These are used to sample a signal at a precise time and hold the value constant during the conversion process.
2   *Analogue multiplexers.* These devices permit one analogue signal out of several to be selected by logical control signals.
3   *Real-time clock.* Signal sampling and construction is often performed in conjunction with an interrupt driven real-time clock. This device relieves the processor of the burden of computing time delays.

7.4   Interrupts

Typically the INput and OUTput instructions of a microprocessor have an execution time of a few microseconds. In the majority of applications, however, the controlled input and output devices (peripherals) operate at a much slower rate: for example, a keypad may be pressed once every few seconds, or a control valve may change state, say, once every minute. It is potentially inappropriate for the microprocessor to continuously monitor the state of the control valve since the microprocessor might then spend most of the time in a non-productive loop, waiting for a change of state to occur, and hence no other processing could be carried out.

Whether or not this is a problem depends on the application; there may be enough spare processor time to permit this inefficient use of the microprocessor. If there is time available, repeatedly examining an input looking for a change of status can be a simple procedure to implement. If there is not adequate time available, a similar effect

Assembly Instructions			Comments
	MVI	A, 02	Initialise PI/0 – Port A input
	OUT	20	Port B output
	MVI	A, 80	
	MOV	B, A	Initialise DAC data.
	MOV	C, A	Initialise DAC test bit.
	MVI	D, 08	Initialise bit count.
REPEAT:	OUT	22	Output DAC data.
	IN	21	Read comparator output.
	ANA	A	Set flags.
	JP	COMZ	Jump if comparator output zero.
	XRA	C	Reset current DAC test bit.
COMZ:	MOV	B, A	Save DAC data.
	MOV	A, C	
	RAR		Update DAC test bit.
	MOV	C, A	
	ORA	B	Set next m.s. bit of DAC data.
	DCR	D	Decrement bit count.
	JNZ	REPEAT	Jump if not zero.

Fig. 7.11 Program Example 7.2

can be obtained by causing the microprocessor to respond to the status of a peripheral directly.

Most microprocessors provide a facility, called an **interrupt**, to enable a peripheral device to inform the microprocessor when it wishes to transfer data. Typically the microprocessor performs some useful processing task until it receives an interrupt signal from the peripheral device. On receipt of the interrupt, the microprocessor temporarily suspends its current activity, performs the required input or output operation, and then returns to its previous task. The

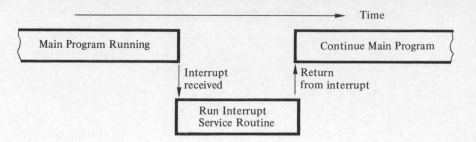

Fig. 7.12   Interrupt service

program which performs this operation is known therefore as the **interrupt service routine** and its activation is illustrated in Fig. 7.12.

In order to implement this scheme, on receipt of an interrupt the microprocessor must perform a number of tasks:

1   Save the contents of the program counter – usually on the system stack – so that it can return to the correct point in the main program after the interrupt has been serviced.

2   Load the program counter with the start address (the memory location which holds the first instruction) of the interrupt service routine.

3   Run the interrupt service routine.
  Note: a) the first group of instructions in the routine usually saves the current contents (again on the system stack) of those processor registers which are used by the service routine itself. This ensures that the action of the interrupted program is not corrupted. Similarly at the end of the routine these contents are restored.
  b) after the appropriate processing the routine may, if this is necessary, reset the interrupt, to indicate the interrupt has been serviced.

4   Finally, return control to the interrupted program by restoring the saved contents of the program counter from the system stack.

7.4.1   Programming with Interrupts

An important consideration when writing a program which contains an interrupt service routine is the frequency at which the interrupts may be generated and the associated processing time required to service each interrupt. The microprocessor is overloaded if the rate of generation of interrupts is such that there is insufficient time to service them all. It is essential that the microprocessor has sufficient time both to perform its main processing function and also to process each interrupt.

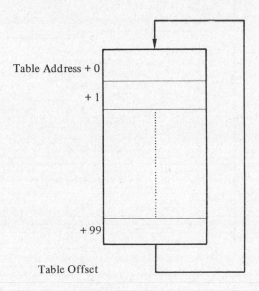

Table Address + 0

+ 1

+ 99

Table Offset

Fig. 7.13 Circular buffer

To ensure that this is the case, it is necessary to estimate the actual run time of each code segment – main program and interrupt service routine(s) – by summing the individual instruction execution times in each segment together. The manufacturer therefore provides the execution time for each machine instruction. Typically, the number of machine clock cycles required to execute each instruction is specified by the manufacturer and hence, because the time for each cycle is known – this is determined by the type of clock crystal being used – it is an easy task to determine the execution time of each instruction.

As an example, consider an interrupt service routine which when activated reads a value from an input port and stores this in a table in memory. Typically, the table may be organised as a circular buffer which always contains the last, say, 100 values read from the port as shown in Fig. 7.13. Assume that the main program continuously sums the values in the table together, computes the average (of the last 100 values), and outputs this value to an output port. A flowchart for the complete program is therefore as shown in Fig. 7.14.

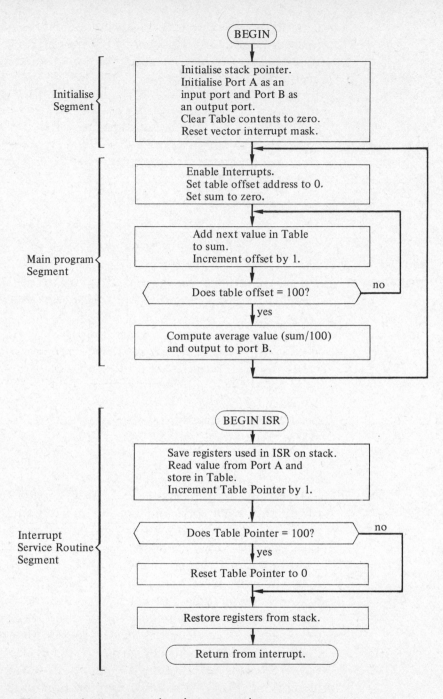

Fig. 7.14 Interrupt service time example

In this example, it is necessary to have sufficient time between interrupts for both the main program to compute and update the average value and also the interrupt service routine to enter each value into the table. Thus if the maximum run time of the main program is, say, 300 μs and the interrupt service routine 200 μs, the maximum rate which the above system could support is one interrupt per 500 μs. As the amount of processing time required in each segment increases – especially if there is more than one interrupt source – the corresponding rate at which interrupts can be serviced will be reduced.

7.5 Multiple Interrupts

The above scheme illustrates the actions which the microprocessor must carry out on receipt of a single interrupt. In many applications, however, the microprocessor may require to control a number of input or output devices each with its own interrupt capability. The Intel 8085, for example, is provided with five separate interrupt input lines. When an interrupt is received, the microprocessor can automatically determine from which device the interrupt has been sent since it is caused to branch to a different fixed dedicated location in memory for each of the five interrupt lines. These dedicated locations are known as the **vector addresses** and for the Intel 8085 are as shown in the table of Fig. 7.15.

Interrupt Input	Vector Address
RST 4.5 (TRAP)	0024 (hex)
RST 5.5	002C
RST 6.5	0034
RST 7.5	003C
INTR	The vector address for this input is not fixed and is part of the instruction placed on the data bus by the interrupting device when the interrupt request is acknowledged.

Fig. 7.15 8085 interrupt vector addresses

Since each interrupt line may be connected to a different device, it is clearly possible for these devices to generate interrupts simultaneously. In order to resolve simultaneous requests, the interrupt lines have a priority associated with them:

RST 4.5 (TRAP)   Highest Priority
RST 7.5
RST 6.5
RST 5.5   Lowest Priority

The TRAP interrupt has the highest priority and is always serviced by the microprocessor immediately it is received. The three remaining interrupts, however, are serviced only when the microprocessor is ready to do so. There are two machine instructions:

EI   (Enable Interrupts)

and

DI   (Disable Interrupts)

which can be used by the programmer to determine when interrupts should be recognised and therefore serviced. Even though interrupts may be enabled, it is additionally possible for the programmer to individually mask each of these interrupts and therefore prevent them from interrupting the processor. This is used, for example, if it is necessary to ensure that an interrupt is serviced completely before allowing another interrupt to be recognised. The interrupt enable flag is reset after the recognition by the processor of a valid interrupt.

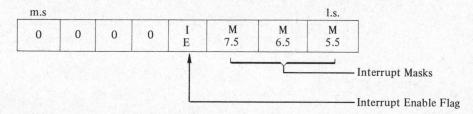

Mask Bit = 1 Disable corresponding interrupt
         = 0 Enable corresponding interrupt

Fig. 7.16 IM-register format

The status of the interrupt enable flag and the three mask bits is held in the IM-register of the processor and its format is shown in Fig. 7.16.

The three mask bits may be set or reset by means of the SIM instruction:

SIM   (Set Interrupt Mask)

The A-register is first loaded with the required mask bits in the three least significant bit positions together with a logical 1 in the fourth bit (mask set enable) and the SIM instruction is then given. For example,

MVI A, 08
SIM

will result in all the mask bits being reset and therefore enabling the three interrupt lines.

Similarly, the status of the mask bits may be examined by means of the RIM instruction

RIM   (Read Interrupt Mask)

After a RIM instruction, the least significant three bits of the A-register indicate the state of the corresponding mask bit.

7.5.1 Interrupt Priority Levels

Since the microprocessor can only service one interrupt at a time, it is necessary for the programmer, when writing each interrupt, to decide the relative priority of each interrupt and hence controlled device. For instance, an interrupt indicating an alarm condition should have a higher priority and hence precedence over the service of an interrupt from a device operating normally.

To illustrate the use of priority assignment of different interrupt inputs, assume the following assignment scheme:

		Priority
TRAP	power failure	HI
RST 7.5	over-temperature alarm	
RST 6.5	real-time clock	
RST 5.5	read new temperature set value	LO

In the Intel 8085 the TRAP interrupt has the highest priority and is non-maskable. This means that it will always be recognised immediately it occurs and is therefore best reserved for catastrophic alarm conditions such as power failure as indicated above. The three other interrupts, RST 7.5, 6.5 and 5.5, may typically be assigned in the order indicated above. This assignment will mean that, if the three interrupts occur simultaneously, the first to be serviced will be the over-temperature alarm, the second the real-time clock (this is discussed in detail in Chaper 8), and finally the read new set value.

If a lower priority interrupt routine has started before the higher level interrupt occurs, the latter will only be recognised when the currently running routine re-enables interrupts (EI) and resets the appropriate mask bit (SIM). It is therefore possible for the programmer to determine when to allow the processor to recognise further interrupts within each interrupt service routine. Hence in the above example, at the start of the RST 6.5 service routine, the programmer would typically reset the 7.5 interrupt mask and set the 5.5 and 6.5 masks before giving the enable interrupt instruction. This would then allow RST 7.5 interrupts to be immediately recognised (and hence interrupt the RST 6.5 service routine) but will delay interrupts on the RST 5.5 and 6.5 lines from being recognised. At the end of the routine, the programmer would then reset both mask bits to allow interrupts from either source to be recognised. This is shown diagrammatically in Fig. 7.17 and the instructions to implement it are given in Fig. 7.18.

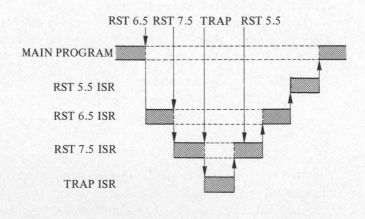

Fig. 7.17 Prioritorised interrupts

Assembly Instructions	Comments
Main Program { BEGIN: MVI A, 08 SIM EI . . .	} Reset all mask bits and enable interrupts
5.5 Interrupt Service Routine { ISR 5.5: PUSH PSW MVI A, 09 SIM EI . . . RET	} Disable 5.5 interrupts and enable 6.5 and 7.5 interrupts
6.5 Interrupt Service Routine { ISR 6.5: PUSH PSW MVI A, 0B SIM EI . . . RET	} Disable 5.5 and 6.5 interrupts and enable 7.5 interrupts
7.5 Interrupt Service Routine { ISR 7.5: PUSH PSW MVI A, 0F SIM EI . . . RET	} Disable 5.5, 6.5 and 7.5 interrupts

Fig. 7.18 Priority interrupts example

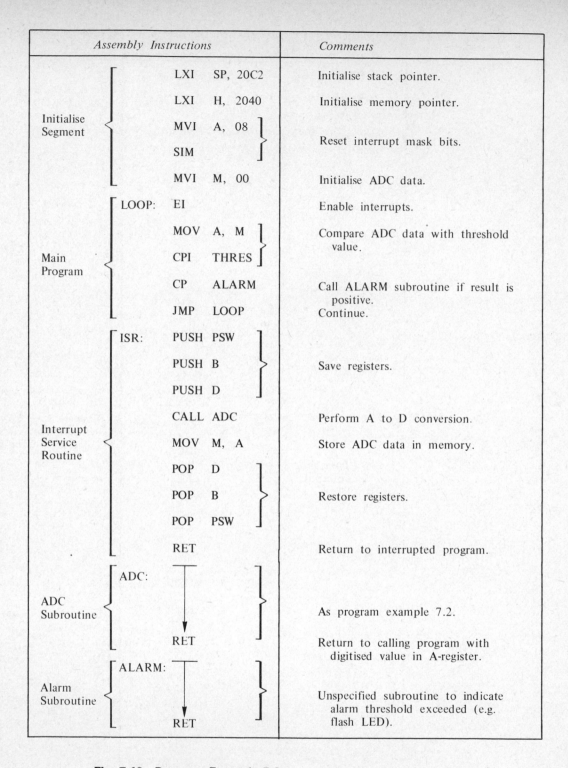

Assembly Instructions			Comments
Initialise Segment		LXI SP, 20C2	Initialise stack pointer.
		LXI H, 2040	Initialise memory pointer.
		MVI A, 08	Reset interrupt mask bits.
		SIM	
		MVI M, 00	Initialise ADC data.
Main Program	LOOP:	EI	Enable interrupts.
		MOV A, M	Compare ADC data with threshold value.
		CPI THRES	
		CP ALARM	Call ALARM subroutine if result is positive.
		JMP LOOP	Continue.
Interrupt Service Routine	ISR:	PUSH PSW	
		PUSH B	Save registers.
		PUSH D	
		CALL ADC	Perform A to D conversion.
		MOV M, A	Store ADC data in memory.
		POP D	
		POP B	Restore registers.
		POP PSW	
		RET	Return to interrupted program.
ADC Subroutine	ADC:	⭣	As program example 7.2.
		RET	Return to calling program with digitised value in A-register.
Alarm Subroutine	ALARM:	⭣	
		RET	Unspecified subroutine to indicate alarm threshold exceeded (e.g. flash LED).

Fig. 7.19 Program Example 7.3

Program Example 7.3: Interrupts

The program example of Fig. 7.19 is intended to illustrate the use of a microprocessor with an interrupt. The program first initialises an area of memory as a stack and resets the interrupt mask bits. It then continuously compares the data returned by subroutine ADC – for example the successive approximate program of example 7.2 – with a preset threshold value (THRES). If this value is equalled or exceeded, subroutine ALARM is called which is assumed, in some unspecified way, to indicate that this condition exists. Analogue-to-digital conversion is performed on receipt of an interrupt on the RST 7.5 interrupt line. The instruction JMP ISR must therefore be stored in memory starting at the interrupt vector address 003C(hex).

Exercises

7.1 Modify the assembly language program of example 7.1 to produce a triangular waveform, both positive and negative ramps.

7.2 Modify program example 7.1 to make the ramp rate selectable by a digital value read from a set of eight switches connected to port A of the PI/O.

7.3 Assuming an average instruction execution time of $3.0\,\mu s$ determine the conversion time of the 8-bit ADC program listed in program example 7.2.

7.4 Modify program example 7.3 so that a LED indicator connected to a PI/O will alternately turn on and then off when the threshold value has been exceeded.

8 Application Examples

8.1 Introduction

This chapter is intended to demonstrate how a microprocessor, with the aid of a number of additional peripheral devices, may be used in a variety of different applications. These applications are dealt with in a simplified way to present application programming techniques in as direct a way as possible. The first two examples are concerned with sequence controllers. The third example is a digital clock for which the microprocessor performs the complete timing sequence and drives a numeric display directly with simple digital outputs. The use of a digital-to-analogue converter is demonstrated in the fourth example which illustrates the use of a microprocessor to generate waveforms typical of those used in many electronic systems. The final example uses an analogue-to-digital converter to monitor the output of a temperature transducer in a microprocessor-based temperature controller.

8.2 Basic Sequencing

Chapter 6 introduced the instructions provided by a microprocessor to input and output logical data to or from an external device and also showed how a programmable input/output (PI/O) port may be used to provide the necessary latching and isolation functions.

In many industrial applications a logical input may be derived from a thermostat, for example, indicating whether or not a certain temperature has been reached, or perhaps a function selection switch on the equipment front panel indicating that a certain mode of operation is required. Similarly, logical outputs may be used to activate a relay which in turn controls the state – ON or OFF – of a pump or heater for example.

To illustrate a simple application of this type, which uses only logical outputs, consider a basic sequencer. Typically, a sequencer activates a number of devices in a preset sequence with a preset time delay between each new device state. For example, a traffic light sequencer changes the state of each light in a set of traffic lights in a preset sequence with a time delay between each state.

A microprocessor is used as a basic sequence controller by switching the appropriate logical output lines on or off – logical 1 or 0 – in the specified sequence with the required time delay between changes computed by the microprocessor.

8.2.1 A Traffic Light Sequencer

As an example of a basic sequencer consider the sequencing of a set of traffic lights. The U.K. sequence is: red; red and amber together; green; amber; red again; etc. The controlled road junction is shown in Fig. 8.1. It comprises the four roads labelled North, South, East and West and a set of traffic lights at each corner (RAG).

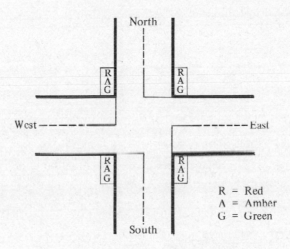

Fig. 8.1 Controlled road junction

The two sets of lights seen by traffic approaching the junction from North and South change in the same sequence. Similarly, the two sets seen by traffic approaching from East and West also change in the same sequence.

The sequence the controller must implement is shown in Fig. 8.2. Note that two different delay times are used during the complete cycle.

Program Example 8.1: Traffic Light Sequence

The sequence of Fig. 8.2 is presented in a computer-compatible form by the state table given in Table 8.1. Note that two flag bits have been used to indicate if the delay following the respective state is delay 1 (D1) or delay 2 (D2). (Only one flag is strictly necessary.) In the table a 1 indicates the corresponding light should be ON and a 0 indicates the light should be OFF.

	North/South			East/West		
	Red	Amber	Green	Red	Amber	Green
delay 1	ON	OFF	OFF	OFF	OFF	ON
delay 2	ON	OFF	OFF	OFF	ON	OFF
delay 2	ON	OFF	OFF	ON	OFF	OFF
delay 2	ON	ON	OFF	ON	OFF	OFF
delay 2	OFF	OFF	ON	ON	OFF	OFF
delay 1	OFF	ON	OFF	ON	OFF	OFF
delay 2	ON	OFF	OFF	ON	OFF	OFF
delay 2	ON	OFF	OFF	ON	ON	OFF

delay 2 (loop back)

Fig. 8.2 Traffic light sequence

Delay 1 = long delay between overall direction changes (~2 mins)

Delay 2 = short delay between transitional light settings (~3 secs)

Table 8.1 Traffic light state table

State	N/S			E/W			Delay	
	R	A	G	R'	A'	G'	D1	D2
0	1	0	0	0	0	1	1	0
1	1	0	0	0	1	0	0	1
2	1	0	0	1	0	0	0	1
3	1	1	0	1	0	0	0	1
4	0	0	1	1	0	0	1	0
5	0	1	0	1	0	0	0	1
6	1	0	0	1	0	0	0	1
7	1	0	0	1	1	0	0	1

The sequencer can be implemented by storing this state table in memory and stepping through it. The appropriate states of the lights are then output, writing the appropriate delay time between steps. This is shown in the flowchart of Fig. 8.3. This flowchart assumes that the most significant three bits of port A of an Intel 8155 PI/O device drive the North/South lights (RAG) and the next most significant three bits drive the East/West lights (R′A′G′).

The delay times are implemented in two stages. With each new state, a delay of D2 is executed and then, if required, a further delay of D1-D2 is executed. (A program implementing this is given in Fig. 8.4.)

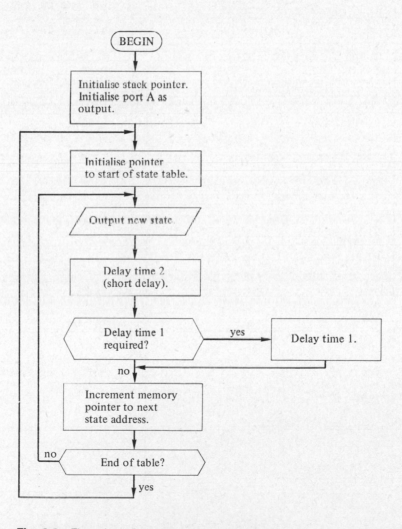

Fig. 8.3 Flowchart for traffic light sequence

Assembly Instructions		Comments
	LXI SP, 20C2	Initialise stack pointer.
	MVI A, 01	Initialise port A as output.
	OUT 20	
SEQ:	LXI H, 2080	Initialise memory pointer to start of state table.
NEWSTATE:	MOV A, M	
	OUT 21	Update state.
	CALL DELAY2	Short delay subroutine.
	ANI 02	Is D1 required?
	JZ NEXT	No: skip D1 call.
	CALL DELAY1	Yes: call long delay subroutine.
NEXT:	INX H	Update memory pointer.
	MOV A, L	
	CPI 88	End of table?
	JNZ NEWSTATE	No: loop for next state.
	JMP SEQ	Yes: loop to start of table.
DELAY1:		
	RET	Delay subroutines similar to those of Program Example 5.3
DELAY2:		
	RET	
2080:	86	
2081:	89	
2082:	91	
2083:	D1	
2084:	32	Table of light states.
2085:	51	
2086:	91	
2087:	99	

Fig. 8.4 Program Example 8.1

8.3 Conditional Sequencing

In some sequencing applications, instead of a change of state occurring after a preset delay, a change of state may be dependent on the occurrence of an external event: for example, water in a vessel reaching a certain level or temperature. This is often referred to as conditional sequencing. The state of an external device can be readily monitored by a microprocessor simply by looping within the program on a particular logical input line waiting for the required change to occur. It is thus possible to use a microprocessor to implement a conditional sequence controller. As an example in the next section a simplified washing machine controller is considered.

8.3.1 A Washing Machine Controller

A washing machine controller is a conditional sequencer which involves both external condition inputs and internal preset time delays. The principles encompassed by this example are applicable to many industrial sequencer applications. The controlled devices interfaced to the logical outputs and the input condition signals for a simplified controller are shown in Table 8.2. A typical sequence of actions for the controller is therefore as given in Table 8.3. This sequence can be directly translated into the state table of Table 8.4. This table is arranged such that the next entry in the table after a state with no time delay is the necessary input condition information.

Table 8.2 Controlled devices and logical inputs for washing machine

Logical outputs	Controlled device
0	Hot water control valve
1	Cold water control valve
2	Water heater
3	Tub motor – wash/rinse speed
4	Pump motor (for emptying tub)
5	Tub motor – spin speed.
Logical inputs	Significance
1	Tub full
2	Water thermostat

Table 8.3 Simplified washing machine sequence

State number		0	Controlled device 1	2	3	4	5	Action
WASH	0	ON	OFF	OFF	OFF	OFF	OFF	Fill tub with hot water until full.
	1	OFF	OFF	ON	OFF	OFF	OFF	Heat water until thermostat closes.
	2	OFF	OFF	OFF	ON	OFF	OFF	Rotate tub at wash/rinse speed for a fixed time D1.
	3	OFF	OFF	OFF	OFF	ON	OFF	Empty tub for a fixed time D2.
RINSE	4	OFF	ON	OFF	OFF	OFF	OFF	Fill tub with cold water until full.
	5	OFF	OFF	OFF	ON	OFF	OFF	Rotate tub at wash/rinse speed for fixed time D1.
	6	OFF	OFF	OFF	OFF	ON	OFF	Empty tub for a fixed time D2.
SPIN	7	OFF	OFF	OFF	OFF	OFF	ON	Spin for fixed time D1.
OFF		OFF	OFF	OFF	OFF	OFF	OFF	Stop

Table 8.4 Washing machine controller state table

State number	Controlled device 0 1 2 3 4 5	Delay/Input D1/1 D2/2	
0	1 0 0 0 0 0	0	0	
	0 0 0 0 0 0	1	0	tub full
1	0 0 1 0 0 0	0	0	
	0 0 0 0 0 0	1	1	thermostat
2	0 0 0 1 0 0	1	0	
3	0 0 0 0 1 0	0	1	
4	0 1 0 0 0 0	0	0	
	0 0 0 0 0 0	1	0	tub full
5	0 0 0 1 0 0	1	0	
6	0 0 0 0 1 0	0	1	
7	0 0 0 0 0 1	1	0	
8	0 0 0 0 0 0	0	1	

Program Example 8.2:   Washing Machine Controller

The controller program must simply step through each state of Table 8.4 and implement the appropriate delay or loop for the relevant condition input. This table approach makes it easy to extend to larger numbers of states and controlled devices.

A flowchart for the controller is given in Fig. 8.5. The logical outputs are assumed to be six bits of port A and the two inputs are connected to port B of a PI/O device as illustrated in Fig. 8.6.

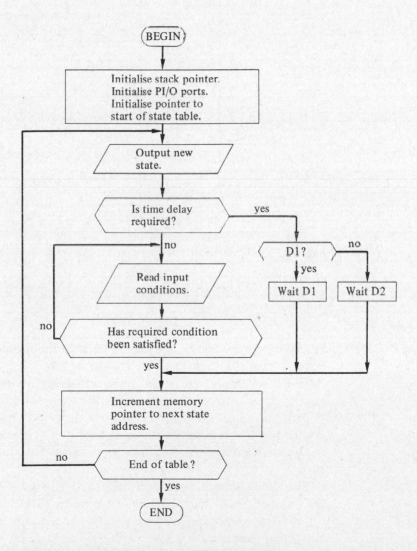

Fig. 8.5 Flowchart for Program Example 8.2

A program corresponding to the flowchart of Fig. 8.5 is presented in Fig. 8.7. The program terminates with a HALT instruction; restarting the program is achieved by a processor RESET with a JMP START instruction at the RESET vector memory address (0000(hex)). RESET is a processor input that causes a response rather like an enabled RST input, except that various processor control functions are reset. It is primarily used to establish the processor in a known condition after the application of power.

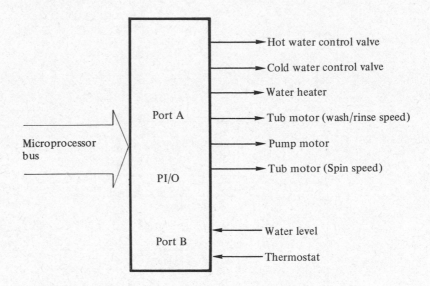

Fig. 8.6 PI/O signals for washing machine controller

8.4 Digital Clock
Many microprocessor applications are concerned with performing specific control functions or actions at preset times throughout the day. For example, an irrigation control system may require a water supply to be turned on at specific intervals, a domestic central heating controller may require a boiler to be switched on at preset times, and so on. A basic requirement for this type of application, therefore, is a real-time digital clock often with a displayed output of the current time.

The delay subroutine described earlier in Chapter 5 demonstrated how a short time delay can be generated with software by executing a number of instructions repetitively in a loop. Although this is a convenient method for generating a single delay, an alternative and better method for generating a continuous timing function is to use

Assembly Instructions		Comments
START:	LXI SP, 20C2	Initialise stack pointer.
	MVI A, 01	Initialise port A to be output and port B to be input.
	OUT 20	
	LXI H, 2080	Initialise memory pointer to start of state table.
NEWSTATE:	MOV A, M	Output newstate.
	OUT 21	
	ANI 03	Is delay required?
	JZ COND	No: skip to conditional section.
	ANI 02	Yes: is it D1?
	JZ D2	
	CALL DELAY1	Yes: compute D1.
	JMP INCM	Skip conditional section.
D2:	CALL DELAY2	No: then D2.
	JMP INCM	Skip conditional section.
COND:	INX H	Increment state table pointer.
COND1:	IN 22	Read conditions.
	SUB M	Test conditions.
	JNZ COND1	Loop until conditions are met.
INCM:	INX H	Point to next state.
	MOV A, L	End of sequence?
	CPI 8C	
	JNZ NEWSTATE	No: loop for next state.
	HALT	Yes: finish.
DELAY1:	↓ RET	Subroutine implementing program delay time D1.
DELAY2:	↓ RET	Subroutine implementing delay time D2.

Fig. 8.7 Program Example 8.2

an additional hardware device called a **programmable timer**. These are now available from most microprocessor manufacturers either as separate devices or combined with other memory and input/output circuits. The Intel 8155, for example, is a single integrated circuit which incorporates a programmable timer with a 256×8 bit static RAM and three programmable input/output ports.

The programmable timer within the Intel 8155 is typical of these devices. It consists of a 14-bit counter which may be programmed to generate either a square wave of a selectable period or a terminal count pulse. The counter operates in the binary count down mode and counts the "timer input" pulses. The initial count length is programmable and when the count becomes zero a pulse is generated on the "timer output" line.

The timer input is normally driven from the microprocessor generated clock and hence, if this has a period of, say, $0.5\ \mu s$, the time interval may be varied up to a maximum of

$$(2^{14}-1)\times 0.5\ \mu s \qquad \text{that is,}\ T_{max} \leqslant 8.1915\ ms$$

The timer may be programmed either to stop after the terminal count pulse is generated or to continue counting and hence generate a new count pulse every, say, 8.1915 ms.

Since the microprocessor clock is normally quite stable, a convenient method of producing a digital clock is to use the programmable timer to continuously generate a count pulse every, say, 5 ms and to connect the timer output to one of the interrupt input lines (RST 7.5) of the microprocessor. The interrupt service routine must then count the interrupts and convert these first into seconds (after 200 interrupts) and then into minutes and hours. A suitable flowchart for such a routine is shown in Fig. 8.8.

The routine uses the following symbolic names which correspond to successive locations in RAM:

COUNT   contains the current number of interrupts since the last change in SECS.

SECS   contains the two BCD digits corresponding to seconds. The contents are incremented by 1 each time COUNT reaches 200.

MINS   contains the two BCD digits corresponding to minutes. The contents are incremented by 1 each time SECS reaches 60.

HOURS   contains the two BCD digits corresponding to hours. The contents are incremented by 1 each time MINS reaches 60.

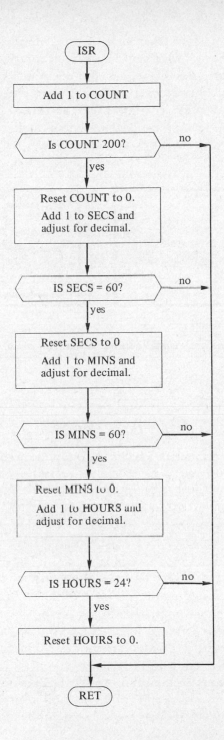

Fig. 8.8 Interrupt service routine

To display the current time in hours and minutes it is possible to use the two 8-bit ports of the 8155 to drive four BCD-to-seven-segment decoder drivers directly. Again these circuits are readily available from a number of manufacturers and can be used to drive a seven-segment LED display. The latter uses an array of seven light emitting diodes (LEDs) to display each decimal digit. The arrangement is shown in Fig. 8.9.

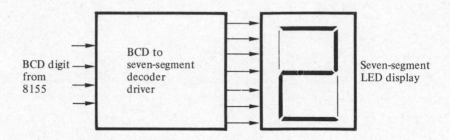

Fig. 8.9   Seven-segment display and driver

Program Example 8.3:   Digital Clock

A program for the clock system can now be written. The program is made up of three parts: an initialisation segment, the main program, and an interrupt service routine.

The initialisation segment is run when the system is first switched on. It initialises the stack pointer and clears the various memory locations used for COUNT, SECS and MINS to zero. HOURS is preset to 12; this gives a simple means of starting the clock after switching on with the clock programmed to start at noon. (Any current time could be preset into these locations by means of a keypad and a short program.) Ports A and B are then initialised as outputs (the timer mode is selected for continuous operation) and the timer count length is loaded to produce 5 ms interrupts. Interrupts are then enabled and the program is run.

The main program simply outputs the current time in hours and minutes via ports A and B, but clearly additional control functions could be included if the clock were only one component of a controlled system.

Finally, the interrupt service routine implements the flowchart shown in Fig. 8.8 and simply updates the current time on receipt of each interrupt. The following addresses are used in the program:

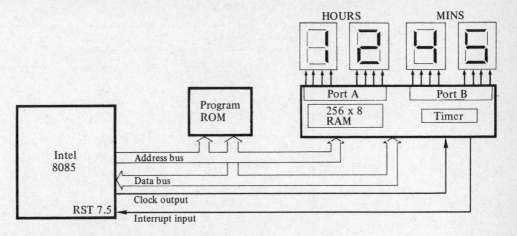

Fig. 8.10 Digital clock schematic

RAM addresses:

20C2	stack pointer
2080	COUNT
2081	SECS
2082	MINS
2083	HOURS

8155 addresses:

Command Register	20 (hex)
Port A data	21
Port B data	22
Low order byte of count length	24
High order byte of count length	25

The program may be stored in any area of memory but an interrupt vector instruction (JMP ISR) must be stored in the vector address corresponding to the interrupt line used by the timer. After the microprocessor is reset, it starts program execution at location 0000. The instruction at this address should therefore be a jump to the start of the initialisation segment. The complete program is given in Fig. 8.11. In any application using interrupts it is important to ensure that interrupts can be serviced at least as quickly as they can be generated. For the clock this means that the interrupt service routine, ISR, must take less than 5 ms to be executed.

Fig. 8.11 Digital clock program

Assembly Instructions	Comments
LXI SP, 20C2	Initialise stack pointer.
LXI H, 2080	
MVI M, 00	
INX H	Clear COUNT, SECS and MINS to zero.
MVI M, 00	
INX H	
MVI M, 00	
INX H	Preset HOURS to 12.
MVI M, 12	
MVI A, 10	
OUT 24	Initialise count length for 5ms interrupts (0.5 μs clock).
MVI A, 27	
OUT 25	
MVI A, C3	Initialise ports A and B as output and timer for continuous operation.
OUT 20	
MVI A, 08	Reset interrupt mask bits.
SIM	
LOOP: EI	Enable interrupts.
LXI H, 2082	
MOV A, M	Load minutes digits into A and output to port B
OUT 22	
INX H	
MOV A, M	Load hours digits into A and output to port A
OUT 21	
JMP LOOP	
ISR: PUSH PSW	Save register contents.
PUSH H	
LXI H, 2080	Add 1 to COUNT
INR M	

Initialise Segment (bracket for first group of instructions)

Main Program (bracket for LOOP through JMP LOOP)

	MVI	A, C8	⎤	Is COUNT = 200?
	CMP	M	⎬	
	JNZ	END	⎦	No: END
	MVI	M, 00		Yes: reset COUNT to zero.
	INX	H	⎤	
	MOV	A, M		
	INR	A	⎬	Add 1 to SECS and adjust. for decimal.
	DAA			
	MOV	M, A	⎦	
	MVI	A, 60	⎤	Is SECS = 60?
	CMP	M	⎦	
	JNZ	END		No: END
	MVI	M, 00		Yes: reset SECS to zero.
Interrupt Service Routine	INX	H	⎤	
	MOV	A, M		
	INR	A	⎬	Add 1 to MINS and adjust for decimal.
	DAA			
	MOV	M, A	⎦	
	MVI	A, 60	⎤	Is MINS = 60?
	CMP	M	⎦	
	JNZ	END		No: END
	MVI	M, 00		Yes: reset MINS to zero.
	INX	H	⎤	
	MOV	A, M		
	INR	A	⎬	Add 1 to HOURS and adjust for decimal.
	DAA			
	MOV	M, A	⎦	
	MVI	A, 24	⎤	Is HOURS = 24?
	CMP	M	⎬	
	JNZ	END		No: END
	MVI	M, 00		Yes: reset HOURS to zero.
END:	POP	H	⎤	Restore register contents.
	POP	PSW	⎦	
	RET			Return from interrupt.

8.5 Waveform Generation

The following example has been chosen to demonstrate, firstly, the use of a DAC to convert the digital outputs from a microprocessor into an analogue form and, secondly, to illustrate the use of a look-up table. The latter is used in many microprocessor applications and, in conjunction with the piecewise linearisation algorithm also described, is a particularly useful technique.

The generation of a repetitive sawtooth waveform using a simple binary counter and a DAC was described in Program Example 7.1. The A-register within the microprocessor was used as a counter and its contents were incremented by unity within a program loop. The contents were output to the DAC after each count increment.

Alternative waveforms may be readily produced by using the contents of the counter, not to drive the DAC directly but instead to provide addresses to successive memory locations, the contents of which store the required digital value which is to be output to the DAC. The contents of the block of successive memory locations used in this way are often referred to as a table and this procedure as a table loop-up process. This is illustrated in Fig. 8.12.

To illustrate the above process, consider the generation of a sinewave. Since the A-register contains 8 bits there are 2^8 or 256 count states. Similarly, assume that the DAC also has 8 bits, and consequently the 8-bit digitised values corresponding to each of the 256 count states are first determined and stored in a table comprising 256 successive locations in memory as indicated in Fig. 8.13.

A repetitive sinewave can then be generated by simply incrementing the contents of the A-register by unity in a program loop, and using the contents as an offset address to find the corresponding digitised value in the table, which is then output to the DAC.

Program Example 8.4: Waveform Generation

The following program example generates a repetitive sinewave using a table look-up process. The table is stored in memory starting at address 2000 and register pair HL is initialised to this value. Register L is then used as the 8-bit counter and the combined contents of register pair HL therefore provides the complete 16-bit memory address automatically. Moreover, on reaching FF, the contents of register L will return to 00 and hence the combined contents of HL will return to 2000 and the process will repeat. See Fig. 8.14 for program.

It is clearly possible to extend the size of the table should greater resolution be required and use, for example, a combined register pair as a counter. For many applications, however, it is possible to reduce the number of look-up values (and hence the size of the table) by using piecewise linear interpolation.

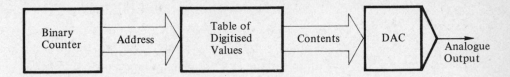

Fig. 8.12   Waveform generation

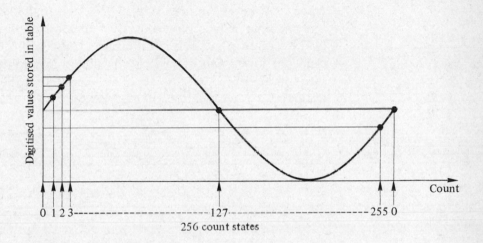

Fig. 8.13   Sinewave table generation

Assembly Instructions			Comments
	MVI	A, 01	Initialise port A as an output port.
	OUT	20	
	LXI	H, 2000	Initialise register pair HL to point to start of table.
LOOP:	MOV	A, M	Look up value from table.
	OUT	21	Output value to DAC.
	INR	L	Increment table offset.
	JMP	LOOP	

Fig. 8.14   Waveform generation by table look-up

8.5.1 Piecewise Linear Interpolation

This involves having a look-up table storing relatively few values spread across the range of the required function. Intermediate values are then calculated by straight line interpolation.

To illustrate this process consider the generation of an exponential waveform using a look-up table containing only 17 values (instead of as previously 256). The function is considered approximately linear between adjacent values as shown in Fig. 8.15.

The 17 stored values are often referred to as *chords* and the fifteen values in between adjacent chords are called *steps*. The fifteen intermediate values between adjacent chord values are obtained by first evaluating the chord difference (that is the difference between adjacent lower and higher chord values) and multiplying this by the step number divided by 16. The complete function value is then obtained by adding this to the lower chord value as in Fig. 8.16.

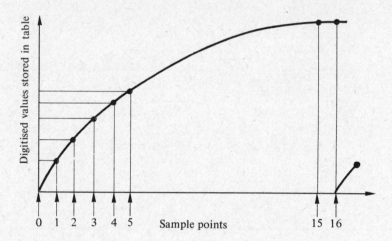

Fig. 8.15 Piecewise linear interpolation

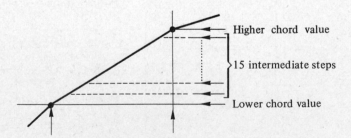

Fig. 8.16 Linear interpolation process

nth intermediate value = lower chord value + chord difference × $n/16$ where chord difference = higher chord value − lower chord value

Program Example 8.5: Piecewise Linear Interpolation

The following program generates an exponential waveform using a table look-up process and piecewise linear interpolation as outlined above. The program does not actually perform multiplication to form each intermediate value, but instead maintains a current increment value (chord difference $\times n$) and simply adds the chord difference to this following each iteration.

In order to maintain accuracy, the current increment value is held as a 16-bit number in register pair BC and the combined contents are divided by 16 to form each intermediate value. This is accomplished in principle by shifting the current increment value four places to the right but, since no shift instructions are available with register pairs, this process is performed in a separate subroutine.

The current increment value is passed to the subroutine in register pair BC and the 8-bit result of the division operation is returned in register A.

Thus, if (B) = 0X (hex) (m.s. 4 bits of B are always zero)

         (C) = YZ (hex)

then   (A) ← result = XY

A flowchart for the subroutine is shown in Fig. 8.17 and the corresponding program is given in Fig. 8.18.

A flowchart for the complete program using this subroutine is shown in Fig. 8.19. The corresponding program for the flowchart of Fig. 8.19 is given in Fig. 8.20. The register usage is:

    HL = Table Address (initialised to 2080 hex)

    SP = Stack Pointer (initialised to 20C2 hex)

    BC = Current Increment Value

     D = Chord Difference

     E = Step Count

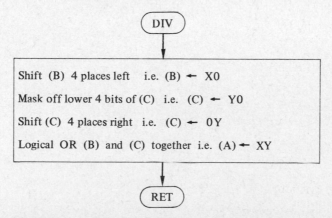

Fig. 8.17 Flowchart for divide-by-16 subroutine

Assembly Instructions		Comments
DIV:	PUSH B	Save Current Increment Value on stack.
	MOV A, B	(B) = 0X
	RLC	
	RLC	
	RLC	Rotate B 4 places left i.e. (B) = X0
	RLC	
	MOV B, A	
	MOV A, C	(C) = YZ
	ANI F0	
	RRC	Mask off l.s. 4 bits of C and rotate 4 places right.
	RRC	
	RRC	(A) = 0Y
	RRC	(A) = (A) OR (B) = XY
	ORA B	Restore Current Increment Value from stack.
	POP B	
	RET	

Fig. 8.18 Program corresponding to Fig. 8.17

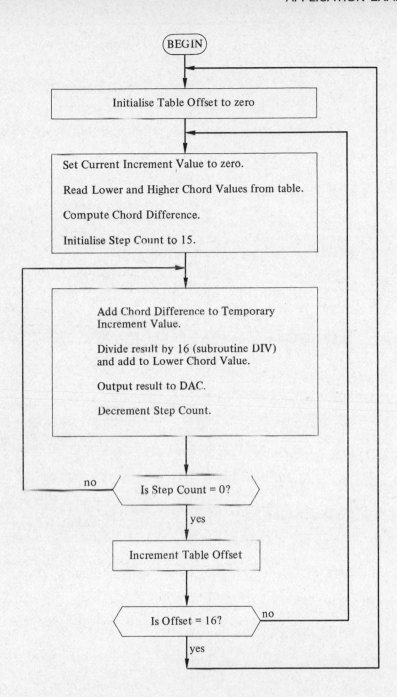

Fig. 8.19   Flowchart for Program Example 8.5

Assembly Instructions		Comments
	LXI SP, 20C2	Initialise stack pointer.
	MVI A, 01	Initialise port A as an output port.
	OUT 20	
START:	LXI H, 2080	Initialise HL to start of Table.
	LXI B, 0000	Clear BC.
CONT:	INR L	Obtain Higher Chord Value from Table.
	MOV A, M	
	DCR L	Subtract Lower Chord Value to form Chord Difference and save in D.
	SUB M	
	MOV D, A	
	MVI E, 0F	Set Step Count to 15.
STEP:	MOV A, C	Add Chord Difference to 16-bit Current Increment Value.
	ADD D	
	MOV C, A	
	JNC NOC	
	INR B	
NOC:	CALL DIV	Divide Current Increment Value by 16 and add to Lower Chord Value.
	ADD M	
	OUT 21	Output value to DAC.
	DCR E	Test if Step Count = 0
	JNZ STEP	
	INR L	Increment Table Offset and test if = 16.
	MOV A, L	
	CPI 10	
	JNZ CONT	No — continue
	JMP START	Yes — reinitialise Table Offset and repeat.

Fig. 8.20 Program Example 8.5

8.6 Temperature Controller

This application example is intended to demonstrate how a micro-processor, with the addition of an analogue-to-digital converter (ADC), can be used as a process controller. A temperature control system has been selected but the principles are applicable to many different processes. A simple ON/OFF control philosophy is used although it is possible to extend this to a more sophisticated proportional or proportional plus integral control algorithm.

The required temperature T_{ref} is assumed to be variable and is stored in a location in RAM. Similarly, the tolerance limits on the required temperature, $\pm\Delta T$, are also assumed variable and stored in a second RAM location. A schematic diagram of the control system is shown in Fig. 8.21.

The controlled temperature is monitored by first deriving an analogue voltage proportional to the temperature – from a thermistor and associated amplifier, for example – and then converting this voltage into an 8-bit digital value by means of an ADC.

The supply to the heater is controlled by a single digital output from the microprocessor via a suitable driver and relay: a logical 1 switches the heater on, a logical 0 switches the heater off. Thus, if the input temperature T_{in} is greater than $(T_{ref}+\Delta T)$ the heater is turned off, whilst if the input temperature is less than $(T_{ref}-\Delta T)$ the heater is turned on. This control action is summarised in the flowchart of Fig. 8.22.

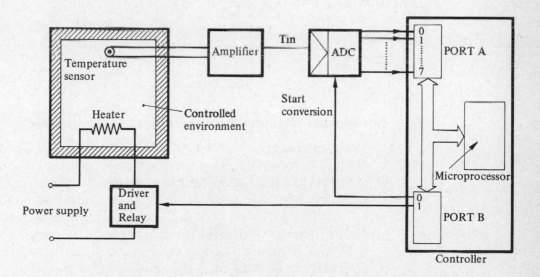

Fig. 8.21 Temperature control system

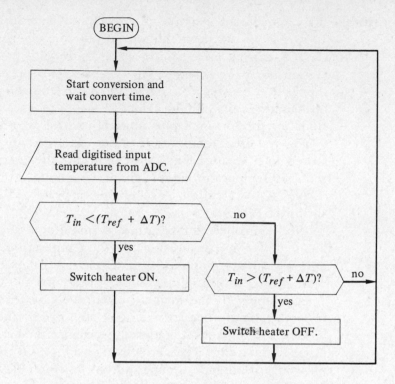

Fig. 8.22 Temperature controller flowchart

Program Example 8.5: Temperature Controller

The program given in Fig. 8.23 implements the flowchart of Fig. 8.22. The required temperature T_{ref} is assumed to be stored in memory location 2080 and the digitised tolerance limit, ΔT, in location 2081. Registers B and C are used to hold the upper $(T_{ref}+\Delta T)$ and lower $(T_{ref}-\Delta T)$ temperature limits respectively and register D is used to hold the current state of port B.

Port A is programmed as an input port and port B as an output port. Bit 0 of port B is pulsed by software to start the ADC conversion cycle and bit 1 is used to drive the supply relay to the heater.

8.7 Summary

The purpose of this chapter has been to illustrate some basic microprocessor application examples and their associated programming techniques. The examples have been presented in a skeletal form without a plethora of refinements which, although necessary in a practical system, mask the essential features of the specific applications.

Sequencers, of which a traffic light controller and a washing machine controller are examples, are widely used in many industrial systems. When implemented with a microprocessor, a sequencer consists essentially of a program which simply steps through the relevant sequence of output states with either a computed time delay between each state – basic sequencing – or a delay whilst the relevant input condition occurs – conditional sequencing.

The digital clock application is in many ways similar. In this case the delay between each new output state is constant and is required to be an exact real-time period. The new output state is thus computed at each step.

A further development of this concept involves converting the digital output states into an analogue quantity. The resulting analogue waveform may be generated from either a fully tabulated set of output states – table look-up – or by using intermediate computation to reduce the table size – linear interpolation – or indeed by fully computing each required output state – Program Example 7.1.

The temperature controller provides an example of an application where the output state is dependent on an analogue input condition.

Assembly Instructions	Comments
LXI H, 2080	
MOV A, M	Read T_{ref} into A and save in E.
MOV E, A	
INX H	
SUB M	Form $(T_{ref} - \Delta T)$ and store in B.
MOV B, A	
MOV A, E	
ADD M	Form $(T_{ref} + \Delta T)$ and store in C.
MOV C, A	
MVI A, 02	Initialise Port A as input
OUT 20	Port B as output.
MVI D, 00	
MOV A, D	Switch heater OFF.
OUT 22	
START: MOV A, D	Recall state of Port B.
ORI 01	Switch bit 0 on
OUT 22	
ANI 02	Switch bit 0 off Start ADC
OUT 22	
CALL DELAY	Wait conversion time.
IN 21	Read T_{in} from ADC.
CMP B	If $T_{in} < (T_{ref} - \Delta T)$, jump to
JC HTON	switch heater on (HTON).
JZ START	

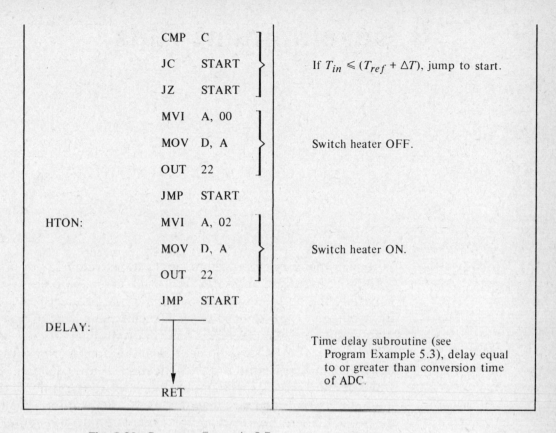

```
              CMP   C       ⎤
              JC    START   ⎬   If T_in ≤ (T_ref + ΔT), jump to start.
              JZ    START   ⎦

              MVI   A, 00    ⎤
              MOV   D, A     ⎬   Switch heater OFF.
              OUT   22       ⎦

              JMP   START

HTON:         MVI   A, 02    ⎤
              MOV   D, A     ⎬   Switch heater ON.
              OUT   22       ⎦

              JMP   START

DELAY:                           Time delay subroutine (see
                                 Program Example 5.3), delay equal
                                 to or greater than conversion time
                                 of ADC.
              RET
```

Fig. 8.23 Program Example 8.5

9 Development Aids

9.1 Introduction

Although many microprocessor applications require only a minimal amount of hardware and software for the actual working system, it is necessary during the development phase of a product to have available both hardware and software development aids. Consequently, microprocessor manufacturers, and indeed many other suppliers, offer a selection of development facilities for microprocessor products. For example, for those applications and evaluation exercises which require only a small amount of software (typically <4K bytes) and input/output facilities, manufacturers usually offer a ready made-up printed circuit board which is a complete microcomputer system. In addition to the basic microcomputer the board incorporates facilities for loading, running and modifying small programs to aid their development.

For those applications which require a significant amount of software, however, it is advantageous to have more sophisticated software and hardware development aids. Consequently, manufacturers also offer complete development systems which contain large amounts of memory for the development of user programs (often >8K bytes), together with system programs and hardware facilities to aid the writing and testing of user software. This chapter firstly describes the facilities which are normally available with single board systems and secondly outlines some of the facilities which are available with a typical microprocessor development system.

9.2 Single Board Systems

The use of a single board system for development purposes has the advantage that the designer is freed from the design tasks required to build the actual microcomputer system and instead can concentrate on the application problems of the overall system.

Fig. 9.1 A single board system (*Courtesy Intel Corp.*)

An example of a single board system is shown in Fig. 9.1. This board is based on the Intel 8085 microprocessor and is typical of such systems. It contains, in addition to the microprocessor, the system clock source, a quantity of read-only memory for holding a system monitor program, a quantity of random access memory for holding user programs, a number of input/output ports, a keypad and associated numeric display, and all the necessary bus control logic.

Although in the final system the application program will normally be stored in ROM, it is advantageous during the development phase for the program to be stored in RAM since it may then be readily changed if any errors are found when the program is executed. In addition, since a typical program (machine) instruction takes only a few microseconds to execute, it is also helpful if, during program development, the rate of execution of the program can be controlled. The monitor program in a typical single board system therefore provides, via the keypad and numeric display, a number of commands to enable the operator to write and store a program into RAM and readily follow and monitor the state of the complete system – the contents of the various microprocessor registers, memory locations and input/output ports – during program execution.

9.2.1   Monitor Commands

Commands to the monitor of the system of Fig. 9.1 are selected by pressing keys on the push button keypad and the response of the monitor is displayed on the numerical display. This response is either an echo of the particular key pressed or a prompt character to indicate that further inputs are required from the user. All the displayed digits are in hexadecimal code and are split into two fields; the left-most four digits are the address field and the right-most two digits the data or contents field. Thus a memory address, for example, is specified by four hexadecimal digits (16-bits) and the corresponding contents by two digits (8-bits).

Typical monitor commands which are available with a single board system are listed below:

Reset
Substitute Memory
Run
Examine Register
Single Step

The **Reset** command enables the user to force the monitor to restart from the beginning of the program. It is used when power is first applied and, after giving the command, the monitor is ready to accept further commands.

The **Substitute Memory** command allows the user to examine the contents of successive memory locations and, if required, to modify their contents. This command is therefore particularly useful for entering a user's program into RAM. The user first writes a program in assembly language form, converts this into hexadecimal form with the aid of a coding sheet (as was described in Chapter 3), and then uses the substitute memory command to load the program into RAM. The substitute memory command also allows the user to modify specific RAM locations – and hence program instructions – if any errors are found in the program during execution.

After a program has been written, coded and loaded into memory, the program can be executed or run using the **Run** (or GO) command. To execute a program which is already stored in RAM, the run key is first pressed, followed by the 4-digit start address in memory of the program. Once a user program is running, the monitor only regains control of the system either if the reset key is pressed or if certain instructions are executed – for example the restart or halt instructions.

The **Examine Register** command allows the user to display and, if required, modify the contents of each of the microprocessor registers. This is a particularly useful facility when used with the single step command since it enables the user to monitor the status of the microprocessor during user program execution and hence can be used to identify possible program errors.

When a program has been loaded into RAM it is usually executed using the run command outlined above. If the program contains errors, however, and does not perform the required task, it is necessary to find the erroneous instructions so that they may be corrected. This can often be a particularly time consuming and, without any software aids, a very difficult task.

The **Single Step** command is such a software aid since it enables a user to examine the state of the complete system as each program instruction is executed. Thus any program instructions which do not produce the required effect may be readily identified. To step through a program which is already stored in memory, the single step key is first pressed followed by the start address of the program. This causes the processor to execute the first instruction but, instead of continuing execution, the program is suspended and control returned to the monitor.

Since control is now with the monitor, before proceeding the user may, if required, examine the contents of the various processor registers and/or memory locations to verify correct operation of the previous instruction. The user may then return to the single step mode by pressing the single step key as before.

9.3 Development Systems

The process of handcoding a program into its hexadecimal form is extremely tedious and time consuming. Moreover, once a program is in hexadecimal form, any errors found in the program during execution often result in a significant amount of modification to the original code. To overcome these problems, manufacturers also provide development systems which contain additional software and hardware to facilitate the development of systems which require in excess of, say, 1K bytes of program.

Fig. 9.2 A microprocessor development system (*Courtesy Intel Corp.*)

An example of a microprocessor development system (MDS) is shown in Fig. 9.2. A typical development system contains, in addition to the microprocessor, a large quantity of RAM (usually >16K), a quantity of permanent storage (normally on dual floppy discs; one for system software and one for user software), a visual display unit for communicating with the user, a printer for hardcopy output, and possibly a PROM programmer for writing developed code directly into PROMS.

System software is the term used to collectively describe the programs which are provided by the manufacturer to aid the development of user (application) programs. Typical system software includes programs to perform the complete translation process from either assembly language to machine code (an assembler), or from a high-level language into machine code (an interpreter or compiler), and also a program to facilitate the modification of programs (an editor).

9.3.1 Assemblers

An assembler program performs the complete translation process of a user program written in symbolic assembly language into its equivalent machine language form. When using an assembler, however, a number of additional facilities are often available to the programmer. For example, it is not necessary to define memory addresses where data is to be stored in absolute hexadecimal form but instead **symbolic names** may be used (e.g. HOURS, MINS, SECS). Thus to increment the contents of a memory location which has the symbolic name SECS, the following code could be used:

```
          .
          .
    LDA   SECS      Increment contents of memory
    INR   A         location with symbolic name SECS
    STA   SECS      by unity.
          .
          .
SECS: DS   1        Define one storage location
                    for SECS.
```

The DS 1 (define storage) statement is used to reserve a single location in memory to be associated with the symbolic name SECS. Alternatively, the same operation can be achieved by using register indirect addressing and the EQUate statement:

```
          .
          .
    LXI   H, SECS   This loads the absolute value
                    2800(Hex) into register pair HL.
    INR   M         Contents of memory location
                    SECS (2800(Hex)) are incremented
                    by 1.
          .
          .
SECS: EQU  2800H    Define SECS to be the absolute
                    value 2800(Hex).
```

Another useful feature is the use of **macros**. If the same list of instructions is required many times in a program, a macro may be defined to specify that block of instructions. Then, each time the same list of instructions is required in the program, only the macro name need be written. For example, a macro, SHIFT, may be defined to shift the contents of the A-register four places right:

```
SHIFT  :  MACRO       start of macro SHIFT
          RRC
          RRC
          RRC
          RRC
          MEND        end of macro
```

Once the macro has been defined, it is then only necessary to give the name SHIFT whenever, say, the contents of the A-register are to be shifted 4 places right.

Since no absolute addresses need be specified in an assembly language program, it is necessary for the user to define the required start address in memory where the translated machine language code is to be stored. This is done by means of the ORG statement since it defines the **origin address** of the program. For example:

```
ORG  2000H
List of program
instructions
END
```

would result in the assembled machine language code being stored in memory starting at address 2000(hex).

The ORG, EQU, DS and MACRO statements are referred to as **assembler directives** or **pseudo-ops** since these are commands to the assembler and do not translate into executable machine code. It should be emphasised, however, that the features outlined here are by no means complete and MDS assemblers offer many additional programming aids. An example of a program listing produced by an MDS assembler is shown in Fig. 9.3.

9.3.2 Compilers and Interpreters

With assembly language, each program instruction has a one-for-one correspondence with the executed machine code and hence the instructions available when using assembly language are determined by those provided by the specific microprocessor being used. Thus, although the instructions of different microprocessors are in many ways very similar, they differ in detail, and consequently a program written in assembly language can only run on those microprocessors which have fully compatible instruction sets.

In addition to assembly language, an MDS usually supports a number of higher-level programming languages. One advantage of using such a language is that the resulting program can be run unmodified on a range of microprocessor systems. Moreover, it is

```
 1:
 2:
 3:                     ; THIS IS AN EXAMPLE OF A PROGRAM USING AN ASSEMBLER . THE
 4:                     ; PROGRAM DETERMINES THE LARGEST VALUE IN A TABLE CONTAINING
 5:                     ; 100 VALUES
 6:                     ; THE PROCESSOR REGISTERS USED ARE :
 7:                     ;     B HOLDS NUMBER OF VALUES IN TABLE
 8:                     ;     C HOLDS MAXIMUM VALUE
 9:                     ; THE MAXIMUM VALUE IS STORED IN THE MEMORY LOCATION WITH THE
10:                     ; SYMBOLIC NAME MAX
11: 2800                     ORG     2800H           ;START ADDRESS OF PROGRAM
12: 2800 0664               MVI     B,100           ;NUMBER OF VALUES IN TABLE
13: 2802 0E00               MVI     C,0             ;INITIALISE (C) TO ZERO
14: 2804 212028             LXI     H,TABLE         ;LOAD TABLE START ADDRESS IN HL
15: 2807 7E       LOOP:     MOV     A,M             ;GET NEXT VALUE
16: 2808 B9                 CMP     C               ;LARGER THAN (C) ?
17: 2809 DA0D28             JC      NEXT            ;NO : JUMP TO NEXT
18: 280C 4F                 MOV     C,A             ;UPDATE (C)
19: 280D 23       NEXT:     INX     H               ;INCREMENT TABLE ADDRESS
20: 280E 05                 DCR     B               ;MORE TO COMPARE ?
21: 280F C20728             JNZ     LOOP            ;YES : LOOP FOR NEXT VALUE
22:                     ;
23:                     ; END OF SCAN , STORE MAXIMUM VALUE IN MAX
24:                     ;
25: 2812 79                 MOV     A,C             ;GET LARGEST VALUE
26: 2813 321728             STA     MAX             ;STORE IN LOCATION MAX
27: 2816 76                 HLT
28:                     ;
29:                     ; THE CONTENTS/USE OF THE SYMBOLIC NAMES USED IN THE PROGRAM
30:                     ; ARE NOW DEFINED
31:                     ;
32: 2820 =       TABLE:    EQU     2820H           ;MAGNITUDE OF ADDRESS TABLE IS
33:                                                 ;DEFINED USING EQU DIRECTIVE
34: 2817         MAX:      DS      1               ;DEFINES 1 MEMORY LOCATION TO
35:                                                 ;HOLD MAXIMUM VALUE ON EXIT
36: 2818                   END
```

Fig. 9.3 An assembler listing

generally easier for a user to write a program in a high-level language since each program "statement" usually translates into several machine language instructions. Examples of high-level languages are PL/M, Basic, Fortran, Cobol and, more recently, Pascal.

The translation of high-level language program statements into executable machine code is often performed by a system program called a **compiler**. In general, compilers are complex programs which require large amounts of memory (>16K bytes) and indeed it is the size of the compilers which determines the quantity of RAM required by an MDS.

A compiler, like an assembler, translates the entire source program into its equivalent executable machine (object) code form. The complete binary coded program is then loaded into memory and run. Compilation, however, is only one of two ways in which the translation process from a high-level language into machine code may be performed. The alternative approach is to use a system program called an **interpreter**.

Unlike a compiler, an interpreter does not perform a complete translation process on the source code before execution but instead executes the resulting machine code as each program statement is translated. The translator program normally used with Basic, for example, is an interpreter rather than a compiler. Interpreters are usually less sophisticated than compilers and can require as little as 2K bytes of memory and, although interpreters of this size do not offer all the facilities offered by a compiler, they are nevertheless very useful software aids. Their major disadvantage is that a program run interpretively executes more slowly than the object code produced by a compiler.

9.3.3   High-level Languages

In general, a high-level language will provide the following development aids:

1   The ability to write single complex arithmetic statements.
2   Powerful control structures.
3   Simple transfer of parameters to subroutines.
4   The ability to define a symbolic name to a data structure composed of a number of variables, e.g. arrays.
5   The ability to assign a variable name to a complex arithmetic expression.

With assembly language it is usually only possible to use arithmetic statements which require only a single machine operation. With a high-level language, however, it is not necessary to break a computation down into its individual components parts and instead it can be written as a single statement. For example,

$$P = (Q + R) - (S + T)$$

is a valid single statement using Fortran where P, Q, R, S and T are all symbolic variable names.

To illustrate the advantage of using more powerful control structures, consider the code required to implement the flowchart segment, shown in Fig. 9.4, used in the temperature controller described in section 8.6. This may be implemented in the high-level language Pascal as follows:

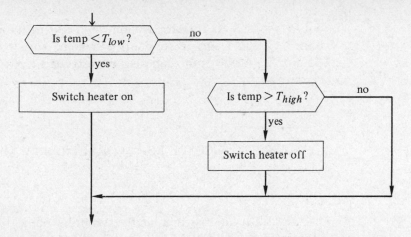

Fig. 9.4 Flowchart segment of temperature controller implemented

———
———

———

IF   TEMP < TLOW <u>THEN</u> HEATER := 1
    ELSE IF TEMP > THIGH <u>THEN</u> HEATER := 0

———

———

Note that, when a condition is satisfied, the corresponding conditional statement is executed and the IF statement is then terminated, thereby bypassing the remaining tests.

The transfer of parameters to a subroutine using a high-level language is also simplified since it is only necessary to include the list of the parameter names with the subroutine call. For example, in Fortran:

———

———

CALL   DELAY   (COUNT)

———

could be used to transfer a value – stored in memory with symbolic name COUNT – to a subroutine which, say, computes a variable delay. Similarly results can also be returned from a subroutine in the same way:

———

———

CALL   COMPUTE   (VALUE 1, VALUE 2, RESULT)

———

———

The ability to assign a single symbolic name to a list of values is illustrated in the following example. The code is in Basic and simply reads 100 values from an input device and stores them in a table which has a single name TABLE:

———

———

```
20    FOR  I = 1 TO 100
21    INPUT TABLE (I)
22    NEXT I
```

———

———

The FOR statement is used to repeat the input operation 100 times for I = 1 to 100.

Many microprocessors provide only the two arithmetic operations for addition and subtraction and consequently it is necessary to write small programs to compute additional arithmetic functions. High-level languages, therefore, often provide previously written sections of code which compute frequently required complex arithmetic expressions. These are known as library functions and it is possible for a user to simply use the function names in normal arithmetic statements. For example, assuming two library functions to compute the sine and cosine of an angle are available, the following type of arithmetic statement may be used:

$$SUM = SIN (A) + COS (B)$$

where SUM, A and B are all symbolic variable names. In addition, users may write their own arithmetic functions and use these in the program as required. Again, these features are only intended as examples of those available with a high-level language.

9.3.4 Editors

When a program has been written either in assembly language or a high-level language, it is entered into the MDS via a keyboard and, for example, a visual display. The latter is used simply to show the user what has been typed and hence what has been input into the system memory. The source program, therefore, appears simply as a string of characters corresponding to each program statement.

The compiler program is then run and this reads and translates each program statement into its equivalent machine language form. If the resulting machine language program does not perform the required task, however, there are clearly errors in the source program which must be corrected.

All translator programs have diagnostic facilities which help the user to identify programming errors. In addition, there is a system program called the **editor** which enables the user to readily modify the source program code. This therefore avoids the user having to revise and type out the entire program again. An editor program is given commands via the keyboard and is therefore said to run **interactively**. Typical editor commands available are:

list   a specified number of lines of source code on the visual display screen

move   to a specified line in the source program

delete   a specified line(s) of code

insert   one or more lines of code

9.3.5 In-circuit Emulators

All the facilities mentioned so far have been programming aids which are intended to help the user to develop and write application software. An MDS also optionally provides a hardware development facility called an **in-circuit emulator** (ICE).

An ICE is designed to emulate the microprocessor being used in the system under development, but since it is itself part of the MDS and therefore under the control of the MDS processor, it is possible to monitor the behaviour of the system under development while it is operating. This is illustrated in Fig. 9.5.

The system under test is often referred to as the **target system** and the ICE behaves exactly as the target processor. It reads the correct sequence of program instructions from the target memory and generates the correct bus signals during their execution. It is hence possible to keep a record, in an area of the MDS memory, of the sequence of actions of the target processor. This record is known as a **real-time**

System under development

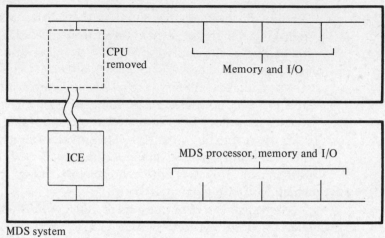

MDS system

Fig. 9.5 In-circuit emulation

trace and it can be examined later by the MDS system software to locate possible errors. The real-time trace can include some logic signals obtained from anywhere in the target system. This is a useful facility for determining hardware faults. The complete sequence usually required to develop a piece of application software using an MDS can be summarised as follows:

1 Design a flowchart which performs the required task.
2 Code the program using either assembly language or a high-level language.
3 Enter this source program into the MDS memory.
4 Assemble or compile the source code to produce the corresponding machine language (object) code.
5 Run the object program.
6 If necessary, debug (i.e. locate errors in) the program using ICE.
7 Edit the source program and return to **4**. until the target system correctly works.

Summary

For those applications which require only a small amount ($<$1K bytes) of software it is feasible to use a single board system for its development. For larger applications, however, it is advantageous to use a development system (MDS).

When using a single board system it is necessary to write all software in assembly language and perform a partial translation process by hand.

When using an MDS, in addition to assembly language it is possible to use a high-level language. This can result in a considerable reduction in program development time.

An MDS also contains an editor program which facilitates the modification of a source program and possibly an in-circuit emulator (ICE) to aid the development of the application hardware.

Appendix 1 The Intel 8085 Instruction Set

The information in the tables in this appendix are reproduced by courtesy of Intel Corporation. The following symbols and abbreviations are used.

A, B, C, D, E, H, L   represent one of the internal processor registers

        M   represents the memory address currently held in register pair HL

    byte   represents an 8-bit (2 hex character) data quantity

    dble   represents a 16-bit (2 byte) data quantity

    addr   represents a 16-bit (2 byte) memory address

    port   represents an 8-bit I/O port address

Register pairs are denoted as follows:

    PSW   represents register pair AF

       B   represents register pair BC

       D   represents register pair DE

       H   represents register pair HL

     SP   represents the 16-bit stack pointer

     PC   represents the 16-bit program counter

The processor flag bits are

    CY   carry flag

     Z   zero flag

     S   sign flag

     P   parity flag

    AC   auxilliary carry

Data Transfer Group

This group of instructions transfers data to and from registers and memory. *No* condition flags are affected by any instructions in this group.

Move

MOV		
	A, A	7F
	A, B	78
	A, C	79
	A, D	7A
	A, E	7B
	A, H	7C
	A, L	7D
	A, M	7E

MOV		
	B, A	47
	B, B	40
	B, C	41
	B, D	42
	B, E	43
	B, H	44
	B, L	45
	B, M	46

MOV		
	C, A	4F
	C, B	48
	C, C	49
	C, D	4A
	C, E	4B
	C, H	4C
	C, L	4D
	C, M	4E

MOV		
	D, A	57
	D, B	50
	D, C	51
	D, D	52
	D, E	53
	D, H	54
	D, L	55
	D, M	56

Move (contd.)

MOV		
	E, A	5F
	E, B	58
	E, C	59
	E, D	5A
	E, E	5B
	E, H	5C
	E, L	5D
	E, M	5E

MOV		
	H, A	67
	H, B	60
	H, C	61
	H, D	62
	H, E	63
	H, H	64
	H, L	65
	H, M	66

MOV		
	L, A	6F
	L, B	68
	L, C	69
	L, D	6A
	L, E	6B
	L, H	6C
	L, L	6D
	L, M	6E

MOV		
	M, A	77
	M, B	70
	M, C	71
	M, D	72
	M, E	73
	M, H	74
	M, L	75

Move Immediate

MVI		
	A, byte	3E
	B, byte	06
	C, byte	0E
	D, byte	16
	E, byte	1E
	H, byte	26
	L, byte	2E
	M, byte	36

Load Immediate (Reg. Pair)

LXI		
	B, dble	01
	D, dble	11
	H, dble	21
	SP, dble	31

Load/Store A direct

LDA addr	3A
STA addr	32

Load/Store A indirect

LDAX B	0A
LDAX D	1A
STAX B	02
STAX D	12

Load/Store HL direct

LHLD addr	2A
SHLD addr	22

Exchange HL/DE

XCHG	EB

Data Manipulation Group – Arithmetic

This group of instructions performs arithmetic operations on data in registers and memory.

Add*

ADD
- A 87
- B 80
- C 81
- D 82
- E 83
- H 84
- L 85
- M 86

ADC
- A 8F
- B 88
- C 89
- D 8A
- E 88
- H 8C
- L 8D
- M 8E

Subtract*

SUB
- A 97
- B 90
- C 91
- D 92
- E 93
- H 94
- L 95
- M 96

SBB
- A 9F
- B 98
- C 99
- D 9A
- E 9B
- H 9C
- L 9D
- M 9E

Add/Subtract Immediate*

ADI byte	C6
ACI byte	CE
SUI byte	D6
SBI byte	DE

Increment/Decrement**

INR
- A 3C
- B 04
- C 0C
- D 14
- E 1C
- H 24
- L 2C
- M 34

DCR
- A 3D
- B 05
- C 0D
- D 15
- E 1D
- H 25
- L 2D
- M 35

Increment/Decrement Register Pair††

INX
- B 03
- D 13
- H 23
- SP 33

DCX
- B 0B
- D 1B
- H 2B
- SP 3B

Decimal Adjust A*

| DAA | 27 |

Complement A††

| CMA | 2F |

Double Add†

DAD
- B 09
- D 19
- H 29
- SP 39

Complement/Set CY†

| CMC | 3F |
| STC | 37 |

Note

* All flags (CY, Z, S, P, AC) affected
** All flags except carry affected
† Only carry affected
†† No flags affected

Data Manipulation Group – Logical

This group of instructions perform logical operations on data in registers and memory.

AND*

ANA—
A	A7
B	A0
C	A1
D	A2
E	A3
H	A4
L	A5
M	A6

ANI   byte   E6

OR*

ORA—
A	B7
B	B0
C	B1
D	B2
E	B3
H	B4
L	B5
M	B6

ORI   byte   F6

Exclusive-OR*

XRA—
A	AF
B	A8
C	A9
D	AA
E	AB
H	AC
L	AD
M	AE

XRI   byte   EE

Compare*

CMP—
A	BF
B	B8
C	B9
D	BA
E	BB
H	BC
L	BD
M	BE

CPI   byte   FE

Rotate †

RLC   07

RRC   0F

RAL   17

RAR   1F

Note

* All flags affected
† Only carry affected

Transfer of Control Group

This group of instructions alter normal sequential program flow. The following condition codes are used:

NZ	not zero	(Z = 0)	PO	parity odd	(P = 0)
Z	zero	(Z = 1)	PE	parity even	(P = 1)
NC	no carry	(CY = 0)	P	plus	(S = 0)
C	carry	(CY = 1)	M	minus	(S = 1)

Jump		**Call**		**Return**	
JMP addr	C3	CALL addr	CD	RET	C9
JNZ addr	C2	CNZ addr	C4	RNZ	CO
JZ addr	CA	CZ addr	CC	RZ	C8
JNC addr	D2	CNC addr	D4	RNC	DO
JC addr	DA	CC addr	DC	RC	D8
JPO addr	E2	CPO addr	E4	RPO	EO
JPE addr	EA	CPE addr	EC	RPE	E8
JP addr	F2	CP addr	F4	RP	FO
JM addr	FA	CM addr	FC	RM	F8

Jump Indirect

PHCL   E9

Input/Output Group

This group of instructions perform I/O operations between the A-register and a specified port.

IN   port   DB
OUT   port   D3

Machine Control Group

This group of instructions manipulate the contents of the stack and alters/controls the state of the processor.

Stack Operations (Register Pairs)

PUSH		POP	
B	C5	B	C1
D	D5	D	D1
H	E5	H	E1
PSW	F5	PSW	F1

XTHL	E3	$(L) \leftrightarrow ((SP))$
		$(H) \leftrightarrow ((SP)+1)$
SPHL	F9	$(SP) \leftarrow (H)$ (L)

Interrupt Control

EI	FB	(Enable Interrupts)
DI	F3	(Disable Interrupts)
RIM	20	(Read Interrupt Mask)
SIM	30	(Set Interrupt Mask)

Processor Control Operations

NOP	00	(No Operation)
HLT	76	(Halt)

Restart Control

RST		
	0	C7
	1	CF
	2	D7
	3	DF
	4	E7
	5	EF
	6	F7
	7	FF

Appendix 2 Binary Multiplication and Division

Since many 8-bit microprocessor applications require only the basic arithmetic operations of addition and subtraction, most 8-bit microprocessors do not have multiplication or division instructions. If multiplication or division is required it is necessary therefore to write subroutines to perform these functions. This appendix presents, firstly, an algorithm for the binary multiplication of two 8-bit numbers to produce a 16-bit product and an algorithm for the binary division of a 16-bit number by an 8-bit number to produce an 8-bit quotient. Unsigned binary number representation is assumed for each algorithm. Secondly, signed binary multiplication is presented.

A2.1 Unsigned Multiplication

The following example given in Fig. A2.1 shows that the multiplication of two 8-bit binary numbers produces a 16-bit product. Each bit of the multiplier is tested in turn, starting with the least significant bit. The operation to be performed as each bit is tested is to simply add the multiplicand – suitably shifted – to the partial (running) product if the multiplier bit is a 1 or to add zero if the multiplier bit is a 0. This is shown in Fig. A2.1.

To implement this process in an 8-bit microprocessor efficiently, it is advantageous to modify the sequence in which the partial products are produced in order to make maximum use of the instructions available. For example, since the final product requires 16 bits, it is convenient to use a combined register pair to hold the accumulated product. Thus, if this is register pair HL and the multiplicand is held in another register pair, the double add instruction can be used to sum each partial product. To obtain the appropriate weighting of each partial product, it is necessary to shift the combined contents of HL as each multiplier bit is tested. This can best be accomplished by

Multiplicand	=	11011011	i.e. 219
Multiplier	=	00110101	i.e. 53
Partial product	=	0000000000000000	
		11011011	Multiplier bit = 1
Partial product	=	000000011011011	
		00000000	Multiplier bit = 0
Partial product	=	000000011011011	
		11011011	Multiplier bit = 1
Partial product	=	0000010001000111	
		00000000	Multiplier bit = 0
Partial product	=	0000010001000111	
		11011011	Multiplier bit = 1
Partial product	=	0001000111110111	
		11011011	Multiplier bit = 1
Partial product	=	0010110101010111	
		00000000	Multiplier bit = 0
Partial product	=	0010110101010111	
		00000000	Multiplier bit = 0
Final product	=	0010110101010111	i.e. 11607

Fig. A2.1 Binary multiplication

Assembly Instructions		Comments
	MVI B, 08	(B) ← 8
	LXI H, 0000	(H) (L) ← 0
LAB1:	DAD H	(H) (L) ← (H) (L) + (H) (L)
	RLC	Rotate multiplier bit to CY.
	JNC LAB2	CY=1?
	DAD D	Yes: (H) (L) ← (H) (L) + (D) (E)
LAB2:	DCR B	(B) ← (B) − 1
	JNZ LAB1	Count zero?
	HLT	Yes: halt.

Fig. A2.2 Unsigned multiplication program

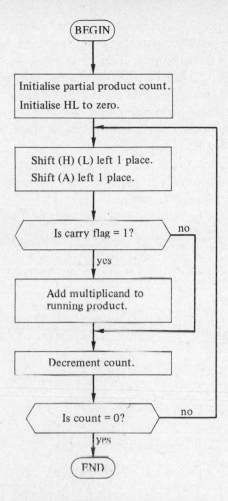

Fig. A2.3 Unsigned multiplication flowchart

testing the multiplier bits starting with the *most significant* and shifting the contents of HL *left* by again using the double add instruction to add the contents to itself ($\times 2$). If the multiplier is held in the A-register, each bit may be tested by shifting the contents *left* one place and testing the carry flag. The complete algorithm is as follows.

Let A   hold the multiplier
      B   hold a count of the number of partial products
    DE   hold the multiplicand – m.s. byte is zero
    HL   hold accumulated product

A flowchart can now be developed, as shown in Fig. A2.3. The corresponding program is given in Fig. A2.2.

A2.2   Division   The division process is analogous to the multiplication process just considered except that, with division, repeated subtractions are performed in place of additions. The process is illustrated by means of an example. The example considered is shown in Fig. A2.4 and illustrates the division of a 16-bit number (the dividend) by an 8-bit number (the divisor) to produce an 8-bit result (the quotient). The first subtraction operation does in fact produce a ninth quotient bit but this is normally zero unless the most significant byte of the dividend is greater than the divisor. To allow for this eventuality, however, the additional (ninth) quotient bit is stored in the carry bit in the program which follows.

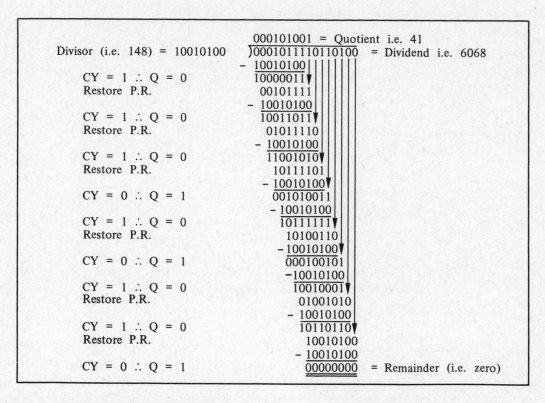

Fig. A2.4   Binary division

Fig. A2.4 shows that the individual quotient bits are determined by subtracting the appropriately shifted divisor from the partial remainder (P.R.). If the result of the subtraction is positive (CY = 0), the divisor is less than the partial remainder, hence the division is correct and the quotient bit is a 1. If the result of the subtraction is negative (CY = 1), the division is incorrect and hence the quotient bit is a 0 and the previous partial remainder is restored. This operation is repeated nine times until all the quotient bits have been derived.

To implement this process with an 8-bit microprocessor it is convenient to leave the divisor in a register unchanged and modify and shift the partial remainder. The result of each subtraction operation can be determined by first complementing the carry flag before testing and then using the state of the flag to form the appropriate quotient bit. The algorithm uses the following register assignments.

Let   AB   hold the dividend – m.s. byte in A

C   hold the divisor

D   is used as a temporary register

E   holds a count of the number of quotient bits.

The quotient is held in the B-register (and hence replaces the l.s. byte of the dividend) with the m.s. (ninth) bit in the carry.

The flowchart is shown in Fig. A2.6 and the corresponding program is given in Fig. A2.5.

	Assembly Instructions		Comments
	MVI	E, 09	$(E) \leftarrow 9$
LAB1:	SUB	C	$(A) \leftarrow (A) - (C)$
	CMC		Complement CY.
	JC	LAB2	CY = 1?
	ADD	C	No: $(A) \leftarrow (A) + (C)$
LAB2:	MOV	D, A	Save A.
	MOV	A, B	Move CY (quotient bit) into l.s. bit position of B and m.s. bit of B into CY.
	RLA		
	MOV	B, A	
	MOV	A, D	Restore A.
	RLA		Move CY into A.
	DCR	E	$(E) \leftarrow (E) - 1$
	JNZ	LAB1	Count zero? No: repeat.
	HLT		Yes: halt.

Fig. A2.5   Division program

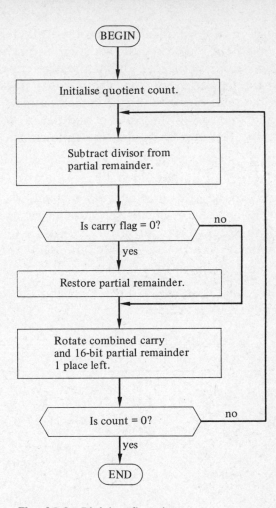

Fig. A2.6 Division flowchart

A2.3 Signed Binary Multiplication

This section describes a program for the multiplication of two 8-bit two's complement signed binary numbers to produce a 16-bit two's complement signed product.

A2.3.1 The Algorithm

The basic multiplication process for two 8-bit positive numbers is illustrated by the example of Fig. A2.7.

Since each multiplier bit can only be 0 or 1, the multiplication process is simply to add the multiplicand (suitably shifted) to the partial product if the multiplier bit is a 1 or to add zero if the multiplier bit is a 0. This process is repeated eight times until all the

```
Multiplicand                          01001001    =    + 73
Multiplier                            00001111    =    + 15
Partial product       =     00000000 00000000
Add multiplicand                      01001001    Multiplier bit = 1
Partial product       =     00000000 01001001
Add multiplicand                     0 1001001    Multiplier bit = 1
Partial product             00000000 11011011
Add multiplicand                    01 001001     Multiplier bit = 1
Partial product       =     00000001 11111111
Add multiplicand                   010 01001      Multiplier bit = 1
Partial product             00000100 01000111
Add zero                      0000 0000           Multiplier bit = 0
Partial product             00000100 01000111
Add zero                     00000 000            Multiplier bit = 0
Partial product       –     00000100 01000111
Add zero                    000000 00             Multiplier bit = 0
Partial product       =     00000100 01000111
Add zero                   0000000 0              Multiplier bit = 0
Final product         =     00000100 01000111     =    +1095
```

Fig. A2.7 Signed multiplication (Example 1)

multiplier bits have been considered. The correct signed 16-bit product is produced.

Unfortunately, the above process does not hold for the multiplication of mixed two's complement signed numbers and certain corrections have to be made to produce the correct signed product. A convenient method for automatically obtaining these corrections is

1 Extend the multiplicand by copies of its most significant bit – 0s if the multiplicand is positive, 1s if it is negative.
2 *Subtract* the final partial product.

This is illustrated, in Fig. A2.8, by an example involving a negative multiplier and multiplicand.

A2.3.2 The Subroutine

Since the multiplicand and the accumulated product both require 16 bits, it is convenient to use two pairs of registers to hold them during the multiplication process. The processor register assignments are

DE holds the multiplicand
HL holds the accumulated product
A holds the multiplier
B holds the bit count

Multiplicand		11111111 10110111	= –73 (extended by copies
Multiplier		11110001	= –15 of its m.s. bit)
Partial product	=	00000000 00000000	
Add multiplicand		11111111 10110111	Multiplier bit = 1
Partial product	=	11111111 10110111	
Add zero		00000000 0000000	Multiplier bit = 0
Partial product	=	11111111 10110111	
Add zero		00000000 0000000	Multiplier bit = 0
Partial product	=	11111111 10110111	
Add zero		00000000 00000	Multiplier bit = 0
Partial product	=	11111111 10110111	
Add multiplicand		11111011 0111	Multiplier bit = 1
Partial product	=	11111011 00100111	
Add multiplicand		11110110 111	Multiplier bit = 1
Partial product	=	11110010 00000111	
Add multiplicand		11101101 11	Multiplier bit = 1
Partial product	=	11011111 11000111	
Subtract multiplicand		11011011 1	Multiplier bit = 1
Final product	=	00000100 01000111	= +1095

Fig. A2.8 Signed multiplication (Example 2)

The multiplication process used in the program is slightly different from that described above in that the partial products are produced in the reverse order and start with the most significant. This has been done because, in the Intel 8085, the contents of a register pair can only be shifted left. This is accomplished by using the double add instruction to add the contents of the register pair to itself.

The HL register pair is also used as a parameter passing mechanism when the subroutine is entered. The contents of HL point to the area of memory where the multiplicand and the multiplier are stored and, on leaving the subroutine, the product is stored immediately following these values as illustrated in Fig. A2.9.

A flowchart for the algorithm is given in Fig. A2.10 and the corresponding assembly language subroutine shown in Fig. A2.11.

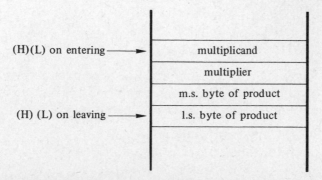

Fig. A2.9 Memory pointer use

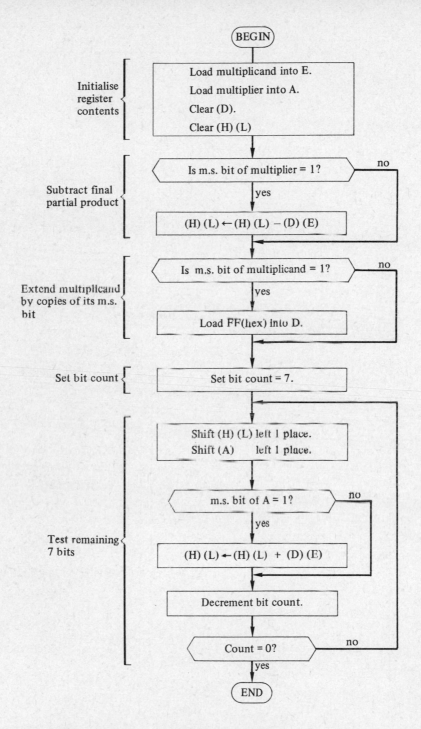

Fig. A2.10 Signed multiplication flowchart

Assembly Instructions	Comments
MULT: PUSH PSW PUSH B PUSH D	Save register contents.
MOV E, M MOV B, E	Load multiplicand into E and save in B.

INX H
MOV A, M
MOV C, A
	Load multiplier into A and save in C.

PUSH H LXI H, 0000	Save and clear (H) (L).
MVI D, 00	Clear (D).
ANA A JP RPOS	m.s. bit of multiplier = 1?

MOV A, E
CMA
INR A
MOV E, A
DAD D
	Yes - subtract final partial product.

RPOS: MOV A, B ANA A JP DPOS	m.s. bit of multiplicand = 1?
MVI D, FF	Yes – load FF (hex) into D (extend sign).
DPOS: MOV E, C MOV A, B	Restore multiplicand into E and multiplier into A.
MVI B, 07	Set bit count = 7

NEXT:	DAD	H	Shift (H) (L) left 1 place.
	RLC		Shift (A) left 1 place.
	ANA	A	
	JP	ZERO	m.s. bit A = 1?
	DAD	D	Yes — add multiplicand.
ZERO:	DCR	B	Decrement count.
	JNZ	NEXT	Branch back if count not zero.
	XCHG		Save product in DE.
	POP	H	Restore memory pointer.
	INX	H	Increment.
	MOV	M, D	
	INX		Store product in memory.
	MOV	M, E	
	POP	D	
	POP	B	Restore register contents.
	POP	PSW	
	RET		Return.

Fig. A2.11   Signed multiplication subroutine

Appendix 3 Microprocessor Characteristics

In order to avoid describing the many small differences between one type of microprocessor and another, the main body of the text has concentrated on a single popular microprocessor system – the Intel 8085. It is thus possible to illustrate simply the fundamental characteristics which are applicable to any microprocessor: the techniques for programming one device apply, in general, to any other type. This appendix has been included, however, to give a brief summary of the main features of some of the other popular microprocessors which are currently available and, where appropriate, to indicate how they differ from the Intel 8085.

It is convenient to break other microprocessors into three categories:

1 *Other 8-bit microprocessors* – this includes devices like the Rockwell R6500, Zilog Z80 and Motorola MC6800/9 which require multiple chips – microprocessor, memory, PI/O – to create a microcomputer system.

2 *Single-chip microcomputers* – this includes devices like the Texas Instruments TMS1000, Intel 8048 and Motorola MC6801 which incorporates the microprocessor, a limited amount of memory (ROM and RAM), I/O facilities, and a counter timer on a single integrated circuit chip.

3 *16-bit microprocessors* – this includes devices like the Texas Instruments TMS9900, Intel 8086, Zilog Z8000 and Motorola MC68000 which are large, high-performance chips intended primarily for those minicomputer-type application areas which require either substantial amounts of random access memory (>64K bytes) or more sophisticated computational facilities (16 or more bits, hardware multiply and divide, etc.).

Some of the characteristics of the devices in these categories are discussed in the following sections.

A3.1   Other 8-bit Microprocessors

A3.1.1   Zilog Z80

Although the instruction mnemonics used by Zilog are different from the 8085, the instruction set of the Z80 microprocessor embodies all the instructions of the 8085 (except RIM and SIM) plus some additional instructions. These include bit manipulation instructions which allow individual bits within a byte to be set, reset or tested with a single instruction, and also some block transfer instructions which allow multiple bytes of data to be moved from one area of memory to another. In addition, the Z80 contains over twice the number of internal processor registers as the 8085, mainly organised as an alternative register set. These are shown in Fig. A3.1.

Although the complete instruction set operates with the main block of registers, it is possible to exchange the contents of the two sets with just two instructions. Hence an interrupt service routine, for example, can use one set of registers for data manipulation whilst the main program uses the other set.

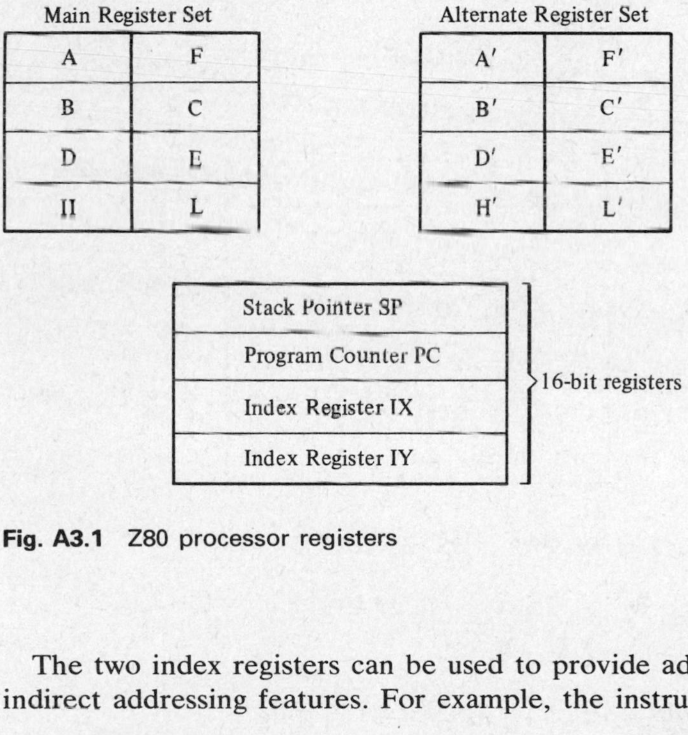

Main Register Set

A	F
B	C
D	E
H	L

Alternate Register Set

A'	F'
B'	C'
D'	E'
H'	L'

Stack Pointer SP
Program Counter PC
Index Register IX
Index Register IY

16-bit registers

Fig. A3.1   Z80 processor registers

The two index registers can be used to provide additional register indirect addressing features. For example, the instruction

LD(IX + 6), C

results in the contents of register C being stored in the memory location whose address is the current contents of the 16-bit index register IX plus 6.

The Z80 also has available additional relative jump instructions. These are particularly useful since they allow the programmer to define a destination branch address relative (± 128) to the jump instruction itself and hence a program segment employing only relative jumps can be relocated without affecting its operation.

A3.1.2   Motorola MC6800/9

The MC6809 is a development of the earlier MC6800. Like the Z80 it has two 16-bit index registers and two separate 16-bit stack pointer registers. The latter are used in the conventional manner but are useful when the system contains two types of program – a system program and a user program. Each program may then use a separately defined area of memory as a stack.

Like the earlier 6800, the 6809 employs only two 8-bit working registers but the instruction set includes some 16-bit instructions and also an unsigned 8×8 bit multiply instruction which produces a 16-bit product. It also has available extensive relative addressing instructions to allow the programmer to write position-independent code.

A summary of the MC6809 register set is shown in Fig. A3.2.

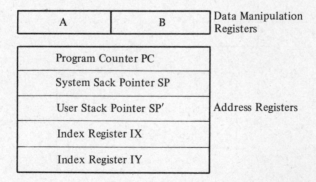

Fig. A3.2   MC6809 processor registers

A3.2   Single-chip Microcomputers

A3.2.1   Intel 8048 Family

The 8048 family encompasses a number of devices with from 1K to 4K bytes of program ROM or EPROM and 64 to 256 bytes of RAM on the chip. In addition, the chip provides three 8-bit I/O ports and a separate timer/event counter.

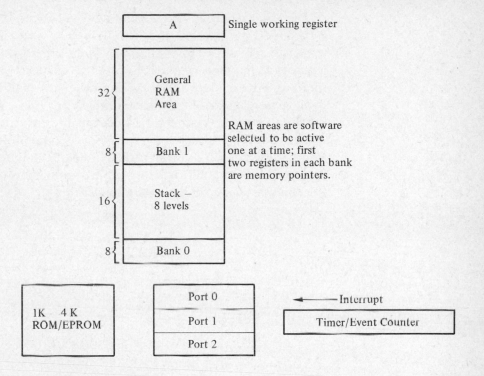

Fig. A3.3   The Intel 8048

The 8048 implements many of the instruction types provided by the 8085 and includes individual bit set and reset instructions. The stack area is obviously limited but can support up to 8 levels of subroutine calls. Similarly, there is just a single interrupt input line. A schematic diagram of the 8048 is shown in Fig. A3.3. Other members of the 8048 family include versions with EPROM in place of ROM for program development and also a device – the 8022 – which has an additional ADC on the chip.

A3.2.2   Motorola MC6801/5

The 6801 is a single chip version of the earlier 6800 with some additional instructions. It contains 2K bytes of on-chip ROM, 128 bytes of RAM, four parallel I/O ports, three serial I/O lines, and three 16-bit timer/event counters. The processor architecture itself is similar to the 6800, consisting of a 16-bit program counter, stack pointer and index register, and also an 8-bit working register. The instruction set is in general similar in character to the 8085 but in addition contains an 8×8 bit multiply instruction.

The 6801 can readily be expanded if additional memory is required by converting two of the parallel I/O ports into memory-space expansion buses. The 6805, however, is a simpler device which cannot be expanded and also has a reduced amount of on-chip memory – 1.1K bytes of ROM and 64 bytes of RAM. It has a single 8-bit timer and a single interrupt input line. The 8601 has two interrupt inputs. A schematic diagram is shown in Fig. A3.4.

The 6805, although instruction-set compatible with the earlier 6800, does not have all the instructions of the latter. It can, however, set, clear or test a bit or byte with a single instruction. It is intended for small size, minimum cost applications.

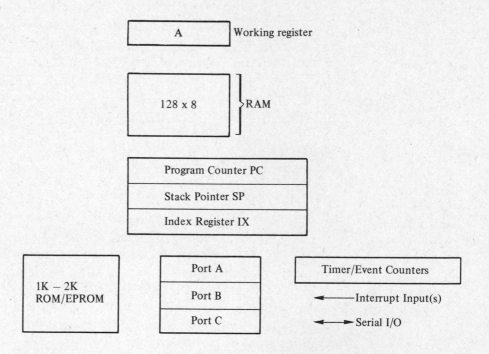

Fig. A3.4 The Motorola 6801/5

A3.3 16-bit Microprocessors

A3.3.1 Texas 9900 Family

The 9900 family encompasses a number of devices with virtually full object-code compatibility across the complete range. The major difference in architecture between the 9900 and the 8-bit 8085, for example, is that the 9900 processor does not include any working registers (A, B, C, D, etc.) but instead contains a pointer – the workspace pointer – to a 32-byte area of RAM which is then used to provide sixteen 16-bit processor registers. This has the disadvantage that different segments of a program must first choose the workspace in memory that contains the appropriate set of working registers used by the instructions in that segment. The major attraction, however, is that it allows rapid switching between a large number of alternative register groups. This is particularly helpful if a large number of different interrupts are to be serviced – the 9900 provides for sixteen levels of priority vectored interrupt. Each interrupt service routine simply switches to its own workspace area thus leaving other workspace areas intact.

The 9900 like other 16-bit microprocessors contains a much richer – more sophisticated – instruction set than the 8-bit microprocessors. For example, the data manipulation group includes multiply and divide instructions, logical and multiple bit shifts, and also instructions to operate on words, bytes or bits.

The 9900 itself is just the processor chip and thus requires external ROM, RAM and I/O circuitry. The 9940, however, is the single-chip version and contains 2K bytes of EPROM/ROM and 128 bytes of RAM on the same chip. The RAM is divided into four 32-byte workspace areas to support the four levels of priority vectored interrupt that can be serviced. The 9940 also provides up to 32 parallel I/O lines and two additional serial-in, serial-out lines. A schematic diagram of this device is shown in Fig. A3.5.

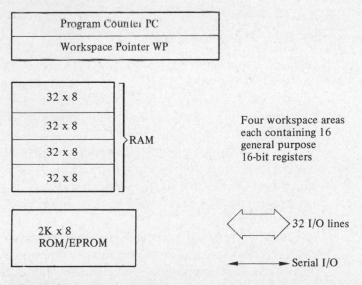

Fig. A3.5 The Texas 9940

A3.3.2   Intel 8086

The 8086 has a directly addressable memory space of 1 megabyte and a rich instruction set. It employs a 6-byte look-ahead (pre-fetch) instruction queue which ensures fast instruction execution times and it is therefore ideal for applications which require either a high system throughput or large memory space (ROM and RAM). The processor is divided into two sections: the execution unit (EU) which contains four 16-bit data (working) registers, two index registers, and two pointer registers; and a bus interface unit (BIU) which contains the 6-byte pre-fetch instruction queue and the relocation register file containing the program counter and four segment registers. The latter can be used by the programmer to set up four areas of memory: a program area, a stack area, and two data areas. Each area or segment can be up to 64K bytes.

While the 8086 is internally decoding and executing the current instruction, the BIU fetches the next sequential instruction – up to 6 bytes – from memory and stores this in the pre-fetch queue. Thus, assuming that the current instruction is not a jump instruction, it is immediately available to the EU upon completion of the current instruction. If the current instruction is a jump instruction, however, the next instruction is fetched from memory in the conventional way.

The instruction set includes 8 and 16-bit signed and unsigned arithmetic in binary or decimal, including multiply and divide. In addition, it contains extensive bit, byte, word and block instructions. A schematic diagram of the processor is shown in Fig. A3.6.

A3.3.3   The Zilog Z8000

The Z8000 is one of the most powerful 16-bit microprocessors (as in the MC68000) with a very advanced architecture comparable with many minicomputers. The processor can address up to 8M words of memory in 64K word segments. A schematic diagram of the processor registers is shown in Fig. A3.7.

The processor maintains two separate types of stack: one for use in special mode by the system's programmer – this is useful, for example, when implementing the system software for sophisticated multi-programming applications – and the other for use as normal user stack pointers.

The sixteen 16-bit general purpose registers can be used either as data registers or as address registers – for example, as index registers.

The data manipulation instructions include signed multiply and divide and can operate on single bits, BCD nibbles (half-bytes), 8-bit

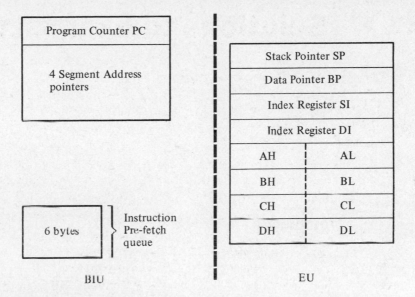

Fig. A3.6   The Intel 8086

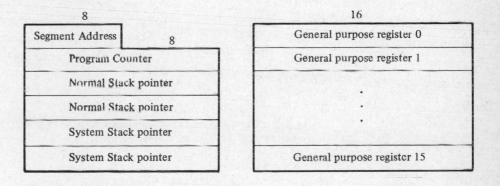

Fig. A3.7   Z8000 register set

bytes, 16-bit words, or 32-bit double words. Similarly, the data movement instructions are very extensive and include a comprehensive set of block and string (group of characters) transfer instructions.

Solutions to Exercises

CHAPTER 1

1.1   35 = 00100011   **1.2**   00010111 = 23
           67 = 01000011   01010101 = 85
       224 = 11100000   11011011 = 219

1.3   27 =   00011011 = 1B (hex)
            96 =   01100000 = 60 (hex)
     3334 = 110100000110 = D06 (hex)

1.4   D3 =   11010011 =   211
         2F =   00101111 =   47
    2D9E = 0010110110011110 = 11 678

CHAPTER 2

2.1 10 bits have 1024 (1K) binary combinations.
     4 bits have 16 binary combinations (0000 → 1111).
  14 bits can address 16K bytes of memory.

2.2 1024 (1K) locations require 10 bits.
     4096 (4K) locations require 12 bits.
      256   locations require 8 bits.

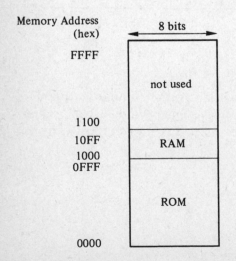

Memory Address (hex) — 8 bits

FFFF

not used

1100
10FF   RAM
1000
0FFF

ROM

0000

2.3 Since the m.s. bits of the address space are not used for memory (ROM or RAM), suitable I/O port addresses are:

1 1 0 0
2 1 0 0
4 1 0 0
8 1 0 0

2.4 $0000 \rightarrow 0FFF = ROM = 12$ bits $= 4K$ bytes
$2000 \rightarrow 21FF = RAM = 9$ bits $= 512$ bytes
$4000 \rightarrow 400F = I/O = 4$ bits $= 16$ ports

CHAPTER 3

3.1

Assembly Instructions	Comments
MVI B, 87	(B) ← 87 (hex)
MOV A, B	(A) ← (B)
MOV C, B	(C) ← (B)
MVI D, 2F	(D) ← 2F (hex)
MOV E, D	(E) ← (D)
LXI H, 8EF2	(H) (L) ← 8EF2 (hex)

3.2

Assembly Instructions	Comments
MVI A, FF	(A) ← FF (hex)
STA 20FF	(20FF) ← (A)
LXI H, 20FF	(H) (L) ← 20FF (hex)
MOV B, M	(B) ← (20FF)
MOV C, B	(C) ← (B)
MOV D, B	(D) ← (B)

3.3

MEMORY		ASSEMBLY		
ADDRESS	CONT	MNEMONIC	OP1	OP2
2000	06			
2001	87	MVI	B	87
2002	78			
		MOV	A	B
2003	48			
		MOV	C	B
2004	16			
2005	2F	MVI	D	2F
2006	5A			
		MOV	E	D
2007	21			
2008	F2	LXI	H	8EF2
2009	8E			

3.4 (2080) = 2A   (A) = 2A
(2020) = 20   (B) = 20
(2021) = 2A   (C) = 2A

21 20 20, 11 80 20, EB, 3E 2A,
77, 3E 20, 47, EB, 70, EB, 4E, 79,
32 21 20, 76.

CHAPTER 4

4.1

Binary	Unsigned Binary	2's complement	BCD
0110 1001	105	+105	69
0010 1000	40	+ 40	28
0111 0110	118	+118	76
1000 1000	136	−120	88
1001 0011	147	−109	93
1000 0111	135	−121	87

4.2
$$
\begin{array}{rl}
103 = & 0110\ 0111 \\
+\ \ 27 = & +0001\ 1011 \\ \hline
130 = & 1000\ 0010
\end{array}
\qquad
\begin{array}{rl}
67 = & 0100\ 0011 \\
+118 = & +0111\ 0110 \\ \hline
185 = & 1011\ 1001
\end{array}
$$

$$
\begin{array}{rl}
105 = & 0110\ 1001 \\
-\ \ 94 = & -0101\ 1110 \\ \hline
11 & 0000\ 1011
\end{array}
\qquad
\begin{array}{rl}
56 = & 0011\ 1000 \\
-\ \ 19 = & -0001\ 0011 \\ \hline
37 & 0010\ 0101
\end{array}
$$

4.3
$$
\left.\begin{array}{rl}
+105 = & 0110\ 1001 \\
-105 = & 1001\ 0111 \\
94 = & 0101\ 1110
\end{array}\right\}
\qquad
\begin{array}{rl}
-105 = & 1001\ 0111 \\
+\ \ 94 = & +0101\ 1110 \\ \hline
-\ \ 11 = & 1111\ 0101
\end{array}
$$

$$
\left.\begin{array}{rl}
+\ 56 = & 0011\ 1000 \\
-\ 56 = & 1100\ 1000 \\
19 & 0001\ 0011
\end{array}\right\}
\qquad
\begin{array}{rl}
-\ 56 - & 1100\ 1000 \\
+\ 19 = & +0001\ 0011 \\ \hline
-\ 37 = & 1101\ 1011
\end{array}
$$

$$
\begin{array}{rl}
103 = & 0110\ 0111 \\
-\ \ 27 = & -0001\ 1011 \\ \hline
+\ \ 76 = & 0100\ 1100
\end{array}
$$

$$
\begin{array}{rl}
67 = & 0100\ 0011 \\
-118 = & -0111\ 0110 \\ \hline
-\ \ 51 & 1100\ 1101
\end{array}
$$

4.4
$$
\begin{array}{rl}
34 = & 0011\ 0100 \\
+52 = & +0101\ 0010
\end{array}
$$

Normal Binary Sum $=$ 1000 0110   CY $=0$, AC $=0$
$\therefore$ Correction $\quad = +0000\ 0000$

Corrected BCD Sum $=$ 1000 0110 $= 86$

$$
\begin{array}{rl}
19 = & 0001\ 1001 \\
+27 = & +0010\ 0111
\end{array}
$$

Normal Binary Sum $=$ 0100 0000   CY $= 0$, AC $= 1$
$\therefore$ Correction $\quad = +0000\ 0110$

Corrected BCD Sum $=$ 0100 0110 $= 46$

$$75 = \quad 0111\ 0101$$
$$-42 = -0100\ 0010$$

Normal Binary Diff. = 0011 0011   CY = 0, AC = 0
∴ Correction   = +0000 0000

Corrected BCD Diff. = 0011 0011   = 33

$$81 = \quad 1000\ 0001$$
$$-39 = -0011\ 1001$$

Normal Binary Diff. = 0100 1000   CY = 0, AC = 1
∴ Correction   = +1111 1010

Corrected BCD Diff. = 0100 0010   = 42

4.5

Assembly Instructions	Action
MVI A, 13	(A) ← 0001 0011
ADI 41	(A) ← 0101 0100
DAA	(A) ← 0101 0100

4.6

Assembly Instructions	Action
MVI A, C8	(A) ← 1100 1000 = -56_{10}
ADI E5	(A) ← 1010 1101 = -83_{10}

4.7

A, B	A AND B	A OR B	A XOR B
A = 1010 1110 B = 0001 0100	0000 0100	1011 1110	1011 1010
A = 0010 1011 B = 1000 1111	000 1011	1010 1111	1010 0100
A = 0011 0111 B = 0100 1000	0000 0000	0111 1111	0111 1111
A = 1010 0101 B = 0101 1010	0000 0000	1111 1111	1111 1111

4.8

Assembly Instructions	Action
MVI A, 9E	(A) ← 1001 1110 CY, P not affected
MVI B, A4	(B) ← 1010 0100 CY, P not affected
RLC	(A) ← 0011 1101 CY ← 1, P not affected
ANI C2	(A) ← 0000 0000 CY ← 0, P ← 1
ORA B	(A) ← 1010 0100 CY ← 0, P ← 0

CHAPTER 5

5.1 The program will loop on the instructions

    LAB1:   DCR   A
                JNZ   LAB1

until the contents of A become zero. The program will then halt.

5.2 The program will loop on the instructions

    LAB2:   INR   A
                JNZ   LAB2

until the contents of A increments up to FF and then overflows to 00. The zero flag becomes set and the program will therefore loop 256 times.

5.3

Let B hold SUM.
    C hold INCVAL.

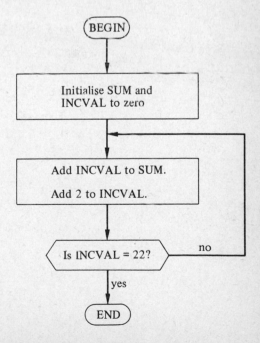

Assembly Instructions	Comments
MVI B, 00	Initialise SUM and INCVAL.
MVI C, 00	
LAB1: MOV A, B	
ADD C	Add INCVAL to SUM.
MOV B, A	
MOV A, C	
ADI 02	Add 2 to INCVAL.
MOV C, A	
CPI 16	Has INCVAL reached 22?
JNZ LAB1	No: loop back to LAB1.
———	Yes: end; sum in B.

5.4 Let the terminal number count be transferred to the subroutine in the C-register and the resulting total returned in the B-register. The numbers in the following subroutine are then summed together in the *reverse* order:

Assembly Instructions	Comments
. . .	
LXI SP, 20C2	Initialise stack pointer.
Load terminal count in C	
CALL SUM	
Sum returned in B	
. . .	
SUM: MVI B, 00	Initialise running total.
LAB1: MOV A, B	
ADD C	Add number count to running total.
MOV B, A	
DCR C	Decrement number count.
JNZ LAB1	Loop if count not zero.
RET	Return to calling program.

5.5 Let A hold COUNT

B hold LIMIT (passed to subroutine as a parameter)

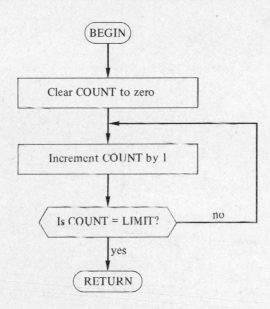

Assembly Instructions	Comments
.	
.	
.	
LXI SP, 20C2	Initialise stack pointer.
Load LIMIT in B	
CALL DLAY	
.	
DLAY: PUSH PSW	Save (A) and (F) on stack.
MVI A, 00	Clear COUNT.
LAB1: INR A	Increment COUNT and compare with LIMIT.
CMP B	
JNZ LAB1	Loop if not equal.
POP PSW	Restore (A) and (F) from stack.
RET	

5.6

Assembly Instructions	Comments
Main Program { ⋮	
Subroutine 1 { TIMDLY1: PUSH PSW ⋮ LXI H, 2081 } MVI M, Limit] CALL DLAY ⋮ RET	Store LIMIT value in memory location 2081.
Subroutine 2 { DLAY: PUSH PSW MVI A, 00 LAB1: INR A CMP M JNZ LAB1 POP PSW RET	As above except COUNT compared with contents of location 2081.

5.7 The maximum run time of TIMDLY2 is approximately 256 times $(00 \rightarrow FF)$ the 7 instructions in the loop. Therefore

$$T_{DLY2} \simeq 256 \times 14 = 3584 \ \mu s$$

Similarly, the maximum run time of TIMDLY1 is approximately 256 times $(00 \rightarrow FF)$ the maximum run time of TDLY2. Therefore

$$T_{DLY1} \simeq 256 \times 3584 \ \mu s$$
$$\simeq 917.5 \ ms$$

Thus the maximum time delay is approximately 920 ms.

CHAPTER 6

6.1

Assembly Instructions	Comments
MVI A, 00	Initialise ports A, B & C as inputs.
OUT 20	
IN 23	Input data from port C and save in register C.
MOV C, A	
IN 22	Input data from port B and save in register B.
MOV B, A	
IN 21	Input data from port A to A register.

6.2

Assembly Instructions	Comments
MVI A, 02	Initialise port A as input and port B as output.
OUT 20	
IN 21	Input data from port A.
CMA	Complement data in A.
OUT 22	Output result to port B.

6.3

Assembly Instructions	Comments
MVI A, 02	Initialise ports A and C as inputs and port B as output
OUT 20	
IN 23	Input data from port C and save in C register.
MOV C, A	
IN 21	Input data from port A.
ADD C	Add contents of C.
OUT 22	Output result to port B.

CHAPTER 7

7.1

Triangular waveform:

Assembly Instructions		Comments
	MVI A, 02	Initialise port B as an output port.
	OUT 20	
REPEAT:	MVI A, 00	Initialise (A) to 00.
LAB1:	OUT 22	Output (A) to port B.
	INR A	Increment (A).
	CPI 00	Loop if (A) have not overflowed to 00.
	JNZ LAB1	
	MVI A, FF	Initialise (A) to FF.
LAB2:	OUT 22	Output (A) to port B.
	DCR A	Decrement (A).
	CPI FF	Loop if (A) have not underflowed to FF.
	JNZ LAB2	
	JMP REPEAT	Repeat.

7.2 The following program reads a value from port A and uses this as a parameter for a delay subroutine (see exercise 5.5). The computed delay is then used to define the basic step duration for the DAC output and hence the rate of the ramp waveform.

Assembly Instructions			Comments
	LXI	SP, 20C2	Initialise stack pointer.
	MVI	A, 02	Initialise port A as input
	OUT	20	port B as output.
REPEAT:	IN	21	Read ramp rate parameter and save in
	MOV	B, A	B register.
	MVI	A, 00	Initialise COUNT.
LAB1:	OUT	22	Output COUNT.
	CALL	DELAY	Call delay.
	INR	A	Increment COUNT.
	CPI	00	Has COUNT overflowed to 00?
	JNZ	LAB1	No: jump to output new COUNT.
	JMP	REPEAT	Yes: read (new) delay parameter.
DELAY:	PUSH	PSW	
	MVI	A, 00	
LAB2:	INR	A	
	CMP	B	Delay subroutine
	JNZ	LAB2	(see exercise 5.5)
	POP	PSW	
	RET		

7.3 The ADC program listed in Fig. 7.11 derives each of the 8-bits of the digitised analogue input by performing the instructions in the loop

REPEAT: OUT   22

.

.

.

JNZ   REPEAT

8 times. The approximate time for each conversion is therefore

$$8 \times (12 \times 3) \ \mu s = 288 \ \mu s$$

7.4

Assembly Instructions		Comments
Initialise Segment	LXI SP, 20C2	Initialise stack pointer.
	LXI H, 2040	Initialise memory pointer.
	MVI A, 02	Initialise Port B as output.
	OUT 20	
	MVI A, 08	Reset interrupt mask bits.
	SIM	
	MVI M, 00	Initialise ADC data.
	MVI A, 01	Initialise LED on.
	STA 2041	
Main Program	LOOP: E1	Enable interrupts.
	MOV A, M	Compare ADC data with threshold value.
	CPI THRES	
	CP ALARM	Conditional CALL to subrt ALARM.
	JMP LOOP	Continue
Interrupt Service Routine	ISR: PUSH PSW	Save registers.
	PUSH B	
	PUSH D	
	CALL ADC	Perform A to D conversion store digitised value in memory.
	MOV M, A	
	POP D	Restore registers.
	POP B	
	POP PSW	
	RET	
ADC Subroutine	ADC: ⎯⎯	ADC subroutine.
	.	
	.	
	RET	
ALARM Subroutine	ALARM: LDA 2041	LED indicator on L.S. bit of port B.
	OUT 22	
	CALL DELAY	Delay subroutine must provide a suitable on-off rate.
	CMP A	
	STA 2041	
	RET	

INDEX